WORKING
—— WITH ——
GOD

*The Ten Modes of
Elevated Leadership*

Dr. Eliyahu Lotzar

Published by

Copyright © Eliyahu Y. Lotzar, 2025
All rights reserved. Printed in the U.S.A.

Tremendous Leadership
PO Box 267 • Boiling Springs, PA 17007
(717) 701 - 8159 • (800) 233 - 2665 • www.TremendousLeadership.com

Tremendous Leadership's titles may be bulk purchased for business or promotional use or for special sales. Please contact Tremendous Leadership for more information.

Tremendous Leadership and its logo are trademarks of Tremendous Leadership. All rights reserved.

No part of this publication may be reproduced, stored in or introduced into a retrieval system, or transmitted in any form, or by any means (electronic, mechanical, photocopying, recording, or otherwise) without prior written permission of the copyright owner of this book except by a newspaper or magazine reviewer who wishes to quote brief passages in connection with a review.

Paperback ISBN 978-1-961202-29-0
Hardcover ISBN 978-1-961202-30-6
Ebook ISBN 978-1-961202-31-3

DESIGNED & PRINTED IN THE UNITED STATES OF AMERICA

*Dedicated to you, dear reader.
With whom else would God work?*

I desire so to conduct the affairs of this administration that if at the end, when I come to lay down the reins of power, I have lost every other friend on earth, I shall at least have one friend left, and that friend shall be down inside me.

Abraham Lincoln, 1864
Letter to a Missouri grievance committee

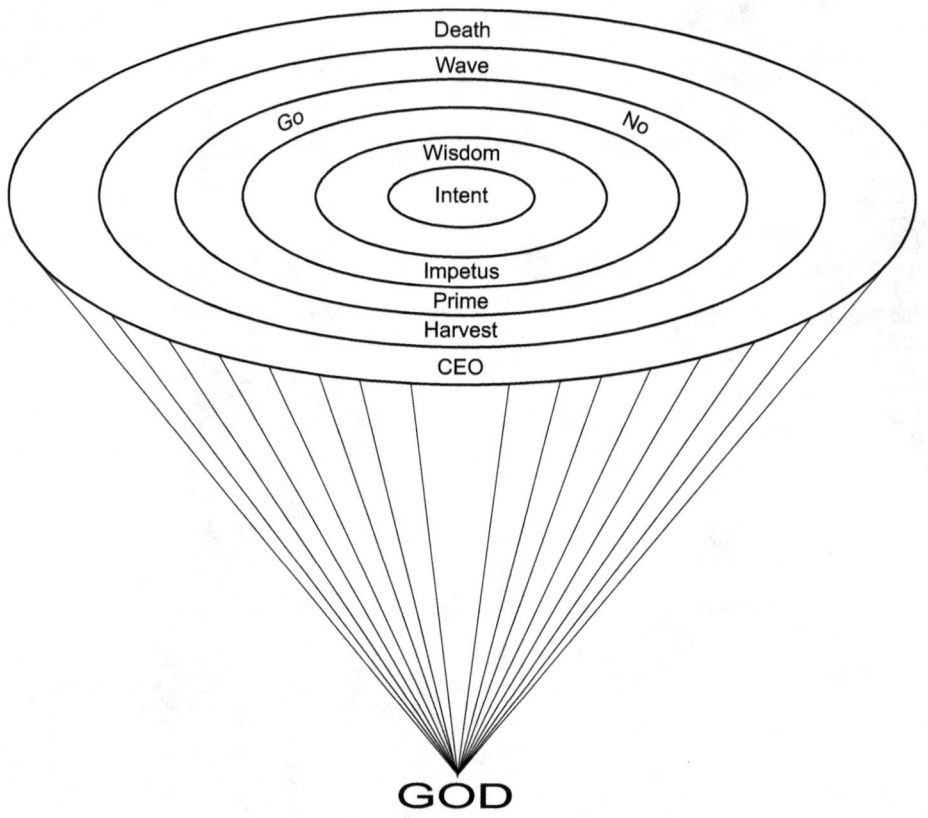

CONTENTS

List of Stories ix
Introduction xi
About This Book xix

Chapter 1: Mode One: Intent 1
Chapter 2: Mode Two: Wisdom. 19
Chapter 3: Mode Three: Impetus. 33
Chapter 4: Mode Four: *Go* 49
Chapter 5: Mode Five: No 65
Chapter 6: Mode Six: Prime .83
Chapter 7: The Door 101
Chapter 8: Mode Seven: Wave. 117
Chapter 9: Mode Eight: Harvest 133

Chapter 10: Mode Nine: Death 149

Chapter 11: Mode Ten: CEO 171

*Appendix A: WHe Built It: CEO Sayings
and Advices* 189

Appendix B: The Working With God Prayer Sheet 195

Acknowledgements 199

About the Author..............................203

LIST OF STORIES

Jeff's Story 4–5
Victor's Story 28
Kimberly-Clark's Story 36
Mark's Story 54
Mark's Story, Continued 79
Gideon's Story 96–99
Kurt's Story 107–110
Mark's Story, Completed 121–124
Kurt's Story, Continued 125–127
Jim's Story 127–131
Jeff's Story, Continued 142–147
John's Story 159–163

Todd's Story 163–166
Wayland's Story 166–168
Ted's Story 168–170
Wayland's Coda 174–176

INTRODUCTION

There are many good books on bringing God into one's work. They give sage advice, highlight biblical principles, and provide examples from the author's life and work. This book also gives some advice and tells stories from the lives of CEOs who work with God, but it is not primarily an advice-giving book or a storybook.

This book is also not moralistic. Many people hear the word "God," automatically jump to "morality," and hold their noses against the stale smell of religious pontification. I take it for granted that you are already moral and also aware that you have room for moral improvement.

No, this book is for you, a leader, to work directly with the Grand Creator Himself. It is my hope that it will help you work with God more efficiently and effectively, with more peace and power. This book is designed to tie you, your project, your entire organization, and God, together.

Investing yourself in establishing and/or strengthening your personal relationship with God will elevate your leadership.

What would it be like to involve God in your work? Or, if you already do that, to involve God more deeply? How would it affect you? How would it change your business? How would it impact your stakeholders?

Working with God may sound interesting, exciting, or even amazing. Or it may sound like career suicide. In any case, a structure to bring God into your business is smart. This book provides such a structure. It provides a tool for the challenge of dealing with God, with yourself, with your business, with God in your business, and with you in God's business.

Why Work with God? (Let's Talk ROI)

Working with God *may* increase your bottom line. It *will* lighten your attitude, expand your viewpoint, and improve the depth of wisdom in your decision-making. It will sometimes bring joy even in turmoil. Working with God will strengthen beneficial attributes such as stability, openness, discernment, and grit. We may or may not put those things as metrics in the annual report, but we do want them.

The extra compassion it brings gives your organizational culture a competitive advantage, as compassion reduces internal friction. Innovative competition increasingly fuels the speed of change. Organizations *have to be* excellent; the days are pretty much gone when a good-enough business is good enough. We demand only excellent, high-performing employees. Compassion, in proper measure and properly placed, brings higher performance to the *team*, not just to the individual.

The race-for-best intensifies a values clash that is already basic to organizational life. On the one hand, we require constantly increasing throughput and consistently better outcomes. Better outcomes are better for the organization and stressful for its employees. On the other hand, we are human; we don't believe operating at a constant '10' stress level is good, and we want to treat employees and consumers as humans rather than as objects.

Gallup polls have shown[1] that employees really want to have a good time at work. They want collegiality, collaboration, and a sense of purpose beyond paycheck. Most people want their time at work to feed their soul, not just fuel their resume or make the owners rich. In the face of organizational decisions based on big data, 'human capital' analytics, remote work, and AI, your staff seeks to humanize their work experience. And that means providing opportunities for them to find meaning at work. In the 1980s, it was *"SHOW ME THE MONEY!!"* Now, the staff's mantra is *"SHOW ME THE MEANING!!"*

You already feed your employees' bank accounts; now, you are asked to feed their souls. They need it and seek it. Of course, to feed their souls, *you* also need to be tanked up with meaning, and you, too, need to feel taken care of.

Being tanked up and cared for is a simple, practical reason to work with God. After all, God does love you, always. Always, always, always, even when you make an 'oops.' Even a very bad 'oops.' God restores your strength by

---

[1] Rothwell, J. and Crabtree, S. (2019). *Not Just a Job: New Evidence on the Quality of Work in the United States.* Lumina Foundation, retrieved on 6/19/2024 from https://www.luminafoundation.org/wp-content/uploads/2019/11/not-just-a-job-new-evidence-on-the-quality-of-work-in-the-united-states.pdf, Charts 9–11.

guiding you in the most efficient paths, as well as while you sleep and do not notice Him. And as for providing meaning, God has readied suits of tailor-made meaning for you and your people.[2]

There are more good reasons to bring God into your work of leadership. First, regardless of how excellent your organizational vision is, God's vision is always *perfect*. He sees what we don't. Second, bringing God into your leadership increases your peace and sense of security. That, in turn, allows you to make wise decisions at higher levels of risk and pressure. Third, God ups your relationship skills by changing how you see and be with others. Fourth, it can be lonely at the top. Wouldn't you like to have a friend who understands you and your situation, never has a selfish motive, and never steers you wrong? You don't always "got this," and even a CEO peer group doesn't always help. God has seen it all, and He loves you dearly. With God, you are never lonely. With God, you are also not at the top. That may sound unpleasant, but in reality, it's a relief. While everyone else sees you on top, you act in the security of His *with-you*-ness.

Lastly, though God is the ultimate friend and helper, our democracies have forgotten His majesty. Today's American is born into a social system that spent several centuries equalizing all manner of creatures, big and small. God is not just your friend; God is the Almighty. Since He owns the company, the land under the company, us in the company,

---

[2] If you haven't read or listened to Rick Warren's *The Purpose Driven Life* (2012, Zondervan Press), I recommend his easy-to-read post-Postmodern statement about how God provides purpose and meaning for life and work.

and the air in us, it's probably wise for us to work with Him. After all, from where does your power ultimately originate?

Why You?

Suppose you believe that God exists or may exist, but religion and/or spirituality make you uncomfortable or semi-uncomfortable. In that case, you have probably invested more of yourself in your relationship to work than in your relationship to God. This book is here to help you put a penny or two on the other side of that scale.

If you are already a faith-filled, God-loving leader, this book can enrich your conversation with God and help you through bad times and good. This book, with its modes, stories, and action steps, will help you 'make the low places high and the high places low so that the glory of the Lord will be revealed' more and more in you and through you at work. Stay tuned.

If you are reading this, you are probably not a committed skeptic.

Why Me?

I coach executives, lead leadership retreats, and design and lead organizational transformation initiatives. I've started and run successful and unsuccessful business ventures. I hold a Doctorate in Executive Leadership with seminal research into employee soft skills that has been continually accessed by commercial, educational, government, and military entities around the globe for years now. Still, many organizational consultants are more accomplished than I am.

But business is only part of the puzzle. For whatever reason, when I was eight years old, the holy God revealed Himself to me. As I looked out over the massive stone platform of what had been God's house in Jerusalem for almost a thousand years, there He was. Though formless, He was overwhelmingly present. He was alive. He was dense and weighty, grand, yet quiet. He radiated and yet contained enormous power. So very ancient, patient, kind. Untouchable yet intimately close, wholly present until there was nothing else. He exuded complete authority. What He conveyed carried more weight than any words anyone had ever said to me, even my parents, who were—or had been, up until that moment—my source of safety, meaning, and truth. When you meet God, you know that He is God.

Moving images across the screen of my mind, God showed me people as they hustled and bustled nearby. They were doing religion—in this case, religious Muslims on top of the temple platform and religious Jews in the plaza below—and regular folk doing their workaday things in the modern part of the city. Maybe with words, maybe heart-to-heart, He told me that people aren't looking to know Him, even many of those who think they are. I could see that they sincerely thought they were looking for Him. Yet, in the depth of truth that mostly only God sees, they were not. They were just being busy doing their best but pursuing matters of their own design.

Some were looking *at* Him or at their image of Him, but none were looking *for* Him. They were busy creating God in their own image, objectifying Him, and thereby objectifying themselves. In the process, they put a veil in front of their minds. Seeing God makes easy sense to a child, but adults have many reasons and commitments that fog their once clear windshield. And how do *you* feel when someone you love deeply doesn't get you?

This book responds to the wistfulness I felt in the Ancient of Days, a love almost like a pain or a sadness. Without much drama, this book offers an opportunity of amazing significance.

God wants us to look for Him. Really. His riches await. He'd love for us to look up for just a moment and knock on His office door. He wants us to come in, have a holy hug, share a meal, peek at the real radiance of life, and go back to our work full of peace and inner joy, focused and ready to share a richer life—of which the workplace is such an integral part.

So here is your opportunity. Do you want to work with God?

ABOUT THIS BOOK

This book describes ten modes. When you familiarize yourself with these modes, you more quickly locate and correct imbalances in yourself, others, and teams. Recognizing that you or others are in any particular mode provides a starting point for you to turn to God in a short prayer: "God, I didn't get what was wrong, but now I do. Show me how to move the team and myself forward."

Use this book when:

- Your decisions have significant ramifications.
- Things aren't working well in your organization or in a part of it. Or when you are doing so well that you risk the ignorance of arrogance.

This book starts with your business. Good news: it *is* about you. The book then moves beyond your business to God's business. Better news: it's *not* about you.

Modes 1-6. The first six chapters bring to life six modes necessary to start and optimize an initiative. That initiative might be a startup, a strategic initiative in a developed organization, or a project. These first six chapters map the modes to organizational functions and provide ways to develop an action-oriented relationship with God. That relationship should help you lead, manage, and keep your business at the peak of its organizational lifecycle.

Having that relationship with God prevents you from being captured by your own favorite values and their blinding biases. It gives God permission to influence your circumstances. He offers *more* than what you normally see. The price? As in a successful human-to-human relationship, you soften your ego. The mature professionals around you will respect that.

Modes 7-10. After you've traveled the first six modes, you reach a door. Beyond the door is *God's* business, *God's* goals. Four modes help you become CEO under God. Go through the door or stay on the road more traveled; it's your choice.

Apply the Action Steps in each chapter and you should feel more connected to God and your business. This connection gives you more peace *and* edge-of-your-seat aliveness. It will also give your business more agility as you move from mode to mode.

Defining "Business"

In this book, "business" refers to any ongoing group that comes together to create value for others. It relates primarily to commercial outfits but also includes nonprofits, associations, government agencies, sports clubs, healthcare organizations, etc. If it regularly organizes people and resources to create value, it's "business."

Defining "Modes"

A mode is a state of operation. A mode is a distinct mental, emotional, operational, and spiritual space hidden in daily life. It's a framework that focuses our perceptions, thoughts, choices, and actions. When we are in a mode, we see, feel, think, believe, and act as guided by that mode. Modes behave as filters in front of our lenses, narrowing and adding color and importance to the world out there. They also connect us with this or that characteristic, or mode of operation, of God. This narrowing allows us to comprehend and act in accordance with a world and a God that is too vast to take in and relate to all at once.

If we are in 'hourly worker' mode, we focus first on how something happening in our environment might influence how many hours we work, how much we get paid per hour, what our supervisor means when she says she expects us to 'go above and beyond,' etc. If we see an employee's behavior as guided by 'hourly worker mode,' we see that their behavior isn't only personal, it's also structural, and that gives us the mental flexibility to create a new structure. For instance, if we entered them into a profit-sharing agreement, their mode would be less focused on 'me and mine.' It would expand to 'us and ours.' That might bring other headaches, but it's an example of how we can use modes to change behavior without the hassles of using carrots and sticks.

Though there is a relationship between organizational culture and modes, which mode you are in changes more rapidly than which culture you are in. When conscious of which mode you are in, you are free to choose to stay in it or move out of it to a more helpful mode. That is why modes are more useful in organizational change than is culture. Practice noticing and guiding yourself through modes. This allows you to see them in yourself and those you lead, giving you leverage.

Modes influence outcomes by increasing or decreasing the perceived utility of various options. Let's say you are that hourly worker's supervisor. They come to you and ask for a raise. If you are in management mode, you might think of the ripple effect on the rest of the staff and the budget you have to deal with. You might say, "Well John, let me think about it," and are stalling for time to find a way to have the least blowback when you say 'no.' If you are feeling for the guy, knowing that his kid was just diagnosed with a treatable but painful and expensive disease, you might be in 'do the right thing for the guy' mode. You might say, "Well John, let me think about it," and, being in that help-the-guy mode, are already thinking of some things you can do to try to get his wages increased, duties lightened, and his schedule made more flexible.

Modes influence others. Anyone new to a department is quickly schooled in who the good and bad guys are outside their new department. It's not far-fetched to have two of your teams be in perennial conflict mode—for instance, sales and legal. Or maybe two teams used to work well together, but a feeling developed in one team that the new executive favors the other and gets them special favors. Team members start assuming that members of the other are selfish, even cutthroat, and maybe even use words like 'idiots.' Those negative perceptions encourage feelings of aloneness and danger. Perceiving danger, they must then protect themselves.

That first team will look out for itself regardless of how inaccurate their original perception of the other team was because they believe their perceptions and thoughts. The other team, naturally, sees the first team protecting itself, and it does likewise—doom loop. Against everyone's better judgement, their time and productive energy are gnawed away as they obsess about others' actions.

Modes are self-perpetuating. Human reality reproduces through the mind's definition of circumstance. Our mode of operation falls under Newton's first law of motion: we stay in the mode we are in until a force of sufficient strength intervenes to change our direction. That's why crime shows look at the criminal's "MO," their *modus operandi,* to predict future behavior.

Sometimes we need external help to see and/or get out of a mode. Because God is omniscient, He always sees another angle. As you build your relationship with God, you develop the ability to hear or feel God and receive His help in moving yourself and others into a more helpful mode. Sometimes that means you must admit something insufficiently good about how you've been leading and change. But it is better to admit it to yourself and change than to suppress it and be accused of it publicly.

Defining God

I've used the word "God" enough by now to have to define the word. This definition is also a bit heady.

The pronoun problem. I refer to God in He/Him/His language. Not "PC," I know. (Then again, neither is mentioning God.) The truth is, I haven't met a theologian who thinks that God is limited to being male. Since God is a unity beyond the material that He created, God encompasses the male/female dichotomy even if He also exists within it.

> *Human reality reproduces through the*
> *mind's definition of circumstance.*
> *Because God is omniscient,*
> *He always sees another angle.*

Then there is the bit about simplicity. You probably don't want me to write "He who is He and She and beyond either He or She" every time I say "He." Also, the Bible refers to God as He (also as They), so when you check out what the Bible says about God (if you do), this book will align. But don't let the gender thing get you stuck. If it is a problem, put a pin in it and keep going.

Why leave such an important point alone? Because of the second, more serious point: God is *so* big that we humans cannot define God.

God is; man slices and dices. Defining anything is saying: "It's *this*, not that." Defining what is as "only this" slices a part from whole-cloth reality. This slicing up diminishes the impact of reality in us, making it possible to handle and ultimately to master. The tactic is very useful. It allows us to rearrange pieces, accomplish things, and change our reality's landscape. As a leader, you know the power of words. Master your words, and you master your reality. Or so it seems.

By separating truth into distinct parts to be able to master our reality, we also distance ourselves from reality itself, which, made by the One, *is* one. The more we master our reality through our traditional habit of understanding, the more we veil ourselves from God's power and radiant glory and His created truth. We think we know. But distanced from actual reality and its Creator, we lose our sustenance and joy. We stop "walking in the garden in the cool of the day" with God.[3] We lock ourselves in our own understanding and seek a God who never left us. Lacking the connection with God and His luscious whole-cloth reality, leaders lapse, tyrants fall, empires break apart, depression, anxiety, anger, insufficiency, and all manner of fears beset us. And, we get stuck in whatever modes we believe will get us back to living in the whole cloth reality with God.

Enough said. If God is, then God is the whole; we are a part, and the part cannot see to define the whole. To work with God, you'll need faith a sincere willingness to check Him out. You'll at least need some smidgeon of emerging faith to see if He is real and will bring you beyond the constraints of your definitions and competing narratives and values. One way to do that is to focus on the unifying modes—in this book, they are "Prime" and "CEO." Another is to train yourself in modal agility, moving from one mode of relationship with reality and God to another mode of relationship with reality and God. This book is designed to help

---

[3] In the biblical account, the first thing God speaks to man is to tell him that all things are permissible for his consumption except that "of the tree of the knowledge of good and evil you shall not eat, for in the day that you eat of it you will surely die." (Gen 2:17 ESV) But in one of the most pivotal moments of the Bible, we indeed eat of the knowledge of good and evil, opposing appetites, and competing values. As a consequence, we immediately no longer see God. Rather, upon hearing Him among us, we hide ourselves from seeing Him: "Then the man and his wife heard the sound of the LORD God walking in the garden in the breeze of the day, and they hid themselves from the presence of the LORD God among the trees of the garden." (Gen 3:8 BSB)

you get modally agile and give you the ability to get unstuck from whatever definitive but limited reality you may be in at any given time. And the living God is always with you to guide you beyond the slices that you call reality. God is the constant of our changing relationships to the changing world.

But to grasp the Constant, you'll need to sit with Him without defining Him, without the intellectual "He is this not that" understanding that is the fruit of the knowledge of good and evil. In Moses' first recorded interaction with God, he asks God to name Himself. God names Himself "*Ehieh Asher Ehieh*," "I Will Be What I Will Be",[4] defining Himself without being defined. God will always be One.

Defining Bible

We can keep this one simple. That this book refers to "The Bible," may be seen by some readers as Christocentric or Judeo-Christian-centric. Aye, 'tis. Though I am familiar with many world scriptures, this book keeps it simple: "The Bible" refers to Genesis through Revelation. If you have fully lived out all that is in those books and still see it as insufficient, I look forward to meeting you.

Business, Modes, God, Bible: What It's All About

It really is all about love. It's about God's business of love, and the love of God's business, and us here together in this big adventure of love.

Let's go.

---

[4]Exodus 3:14

Chapter One

INTENT

•————————• Point B

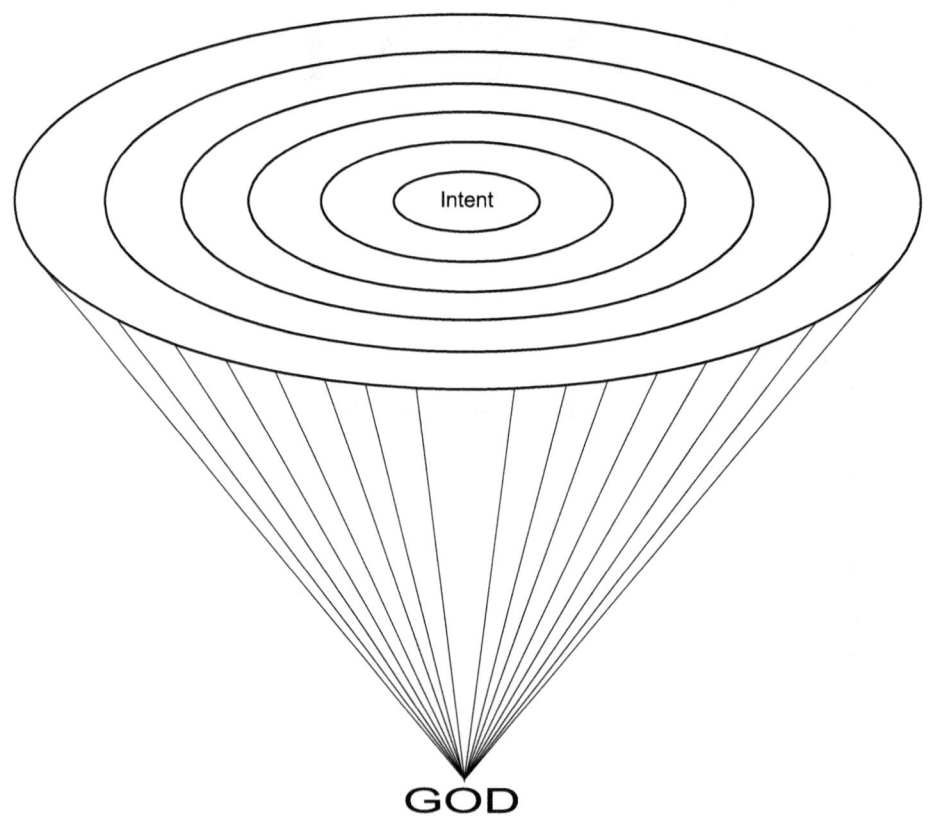

In the beginning was the Word.

John 1:1
(about 2000 years ago)

Presumably, you intend to have more. Maybe you intend to *be* more. Maybe both. Wanting more is intrinsic to life. Just look at the trees. A tree has an insatiable appetite for growth. It is designed for growth; despite challenges brought by storms, drought, and little beetles making lunch out of its roots, the tree inexorably grows toward its fullest expression. It only stops growing when it dies. If a tree could talk, it would tell us that it intends to keep growing.

I've met a number of VPs and CXOs who were CEOs at one time and gave it up because of the crazy pressure of it all. Did they want less? In a way, yes: less risk, less pressure, less stress. But that doesn't mean they stopped growing. They shifted 'downward' because it was time for more: more peace, more happiness, more integrity, strengthened family, more time, more joy.

So the question isn't whether you intend to have or to be more; the question is, what more do you intend to have or be? If your organization, team, or project is to maintain clear intent, you need to be a model of clear intent.

Stop and ask yourself now: What *more* do I intend?

Jeff's Story

Tall, broad-shouldered Jeff Skeen grew up in a military family in a wealthy suburb of Washington, DC. He quickly absorbed athletic discipline and drive. By sixth grade, he knew exactly what he was going to be when he grew up: CEO of a publicly traded company—not a doctor, firefighter, or astronaut; CEO of a publicly traded company.

Jeff was on the success track. Fresh out of school in the 1980s, he was offered a finance job with a $70K base. That was a lot back then. It was in Hollywood, no less, and with a leading perfume producer. Ah, to be a young, sexy, educated, white male in America, having a sexy job in a sexy firm in a sexy city, making good money: life is good! It was obvious to Jeff that he was meant for great things. Taking this job would be the perfect start to becoming CEO of a publicly traded company. Clearly, God was with him.

For whatever reason, God also offered Jeff a humble beginnings option. Shortly after receiving the perfume people's offer, a sweet widower asked him to manage the struggling local office supply store that she and her now-deceased husband had managed into near ruin. He asked how much could they offer him. $18K, she said. *That* did not align with Jeff's intent.

We'll continue Jeff's story later on.

Leading with Intent

Leading is much about, or maybe all about, generating and managing organizational intent. Mission, vision, culture, and strategy help you manage the multiplicity of competing intents you find in your organization; they are tools of Intent.[5] When you generate and manage a set of intentions, you operate in Intent. In Intent, you create direction.

The mode of Intent. Intent is the vehicle through which 'Point B' is created. 'Point B,' like Intent, is a mental construct until it is actualized by work done through the other modes. You begin in Intent, but Intent also produces the picture of the end that guides you through the whole endeavor.

---

[5] As with the other nine modes in this book, when you see Intent with a capital "I," it refers to the mode. When you see intent spelled lower-case, it relates to how we normally use the word: an intention to achieve a particular outcome.

> *Intent is the vehicle through which 'Point B' is created.*

The mode of Intent encourages an appetite for achievement and a desire for motion. It wields immense influence over organizational outcomes. Without Intent, our intentions are just thoughts that meander through the mind. Intent provides the internal environment appropriate for focusing thoughts into a clear desire for a specific more. To flesh that out, do the following Action Step.

Action Step

Take a step back and ask yourself:

A. What are my core intents at work?
B. What intent is for me personally and what is for my company?
C. My organization has its own historical intent—how aligned am I with it right now?

How Intent Works

Beginning with an intention isn't exactly a groundbreaking piece of business insight. But how does it actually work? What are the components of stronger, more focused intent? Let's look deeper to spot whether our people or processes (or we ourselves) are stuck in a battle of intents or are in the normal tensions involved in working out of a common intent.

A dynamism inside intent (and in the mode of Intent) generates movement. The main elements of Intent are:

1. Ideas
2. Division
3. Faith
4. Resolution
5. Identity

Dividing Intent into elements helps us see if we are over- or under-emphasizing the importance of any one element. We will look at each of these elements and then at how God moves us beyond ourselves in Intent.

Ideas generate division. Before you start a business, embark on a career change, or any other project, you have an *idea* of what needs to be that, right now, isn't. That idea creates a destination. You now desire to be somewhere you are not. As soon as you have an idea, you notice that you have not actualized the idea, and you are not living in the future you want. You are now split. You are divided. You live in two places: you are where you are, while part of your mind now lives where you *want* to be or where you believe you *should* be. That is deeply unsettling. But wonderful constructive tension motivates everything in us to say, "I must get there."

Division demands faith. That idea-driven division shows up at work as the drive to get results. You go to work because of hope for the future and with sufficient faith in your ability to get there. As you see, faith exists at work. It may be faith in God, yourself, others, or all of the above, but faith exists plentifully at work. Every time you show up for work—unless you are just going through the motions—your actions are a loud "Amen."

True, "amen" is a word for religious circles. "The word "amen" is a direct transliteration from the Hebrew, where amen's three letters—amn (אמן)—are also the root word in "emunah" (אמונה), or "faith." *Amn* is a state of agreement about something hoped for, seen in mind and heart, but not yet physically apparent. After all, if it were already a fact, you wouldn't need to *believe* it is real. At work, we operate with fact and faith.

The mode of Intent holds the faith that is typically hidden at the foundations of an organization. Intent is the home for vision-mission retreats, strategic planning sessions, and "this I believe" values declarations on websites. Faith in your vision and faith in God are united in the same process. If we have faith that we can heal most of the sick who are about to walk in our door, as the managing director of a clinical practice would, it is not a new process for us to believe that God helps move the project forward: it is the same process of faith. We only see a difference between faith in our ability and faith in God's ability (or reality) because we see our practitioners working and our patient conditions improving. Still, we haven't seen God move a project forward. But the eyes of faith, once pointed toward God, can see God working, just as the eyes of inquiry pointed toward moving leaves can see wind.

The challenge to faith in God is that we have no proof of God's interventions. At least, that is what we have increasingly believed over the past four hundred years, as science and its technological conveniences have narrowed our understanding of what is real to what can be physically demonstrated. If you have a chance encounter with a potential client whom you intended to pitch, was that fate, God, or a random occurrence? In the case of our chance encounter, you have proof of nothing and theories of everything.

Success in any endeavor takes vision at the start and faith in that vision all along.

If you don't place your faith in God, do a thought experiment: for a moment, let yourself imagine that it was God who gently arranged the chance meeting. See that He did it for your sake and the sake of others. After all, He loves you just as He loves others. Then, having for a moment that vision or feeling of God arranging that chance meeting, apply that belief—not fact, but belief in the face of the unknown—to other coincidences. Go ahead; if you are fearless enough, try it now. And if your insides revolt and you don't want to try it, ask yourself what you are afraid of. Find out. Then, ask yourself if that is a real fear, based in fact, or if it is based on yet another belief. Even the thought of encountering God, taken earnestly, is a rich experience of discovery.

You will see quickly enough that one coincidence depends on the occurrence of one or more previous coincidences, and each of those coincidences depends on yet more coincidences, ever on back. In the end, you are left to choose the source of all things. Even if you stand on not knowing, you will still adopt an operational stance to work with God, work with science, work with both, or have faith in nothing, hope for nothing, and work for nothing. Which operational stance serves you and others best? Just ask which one imbues the gamut of human experience with love. Or do you wish to distill love from work and relegate it to 'personal time'? If so, then without love, who is it there who is working? Faith is necessary for work.

Faith sustains tension. Transmitting faith in your idea takes great ability. To transmit faith in your idea, you must overcome cognitive tension between your picture of the future and others' awareness that such a future is uncertain.

Most people believe more in what exists than in what does not exist. Most people don't like cognitive dissonance or being split. Faith may spring up with a new and green hope, but it tends to wither while implementing it through the long summer of circumstances. Sustaining faith in your idea takes great ability and constant vigilance.

Now imagine that the hitherto hidden God was helping you. Imagine God paving the way in investors' thinking, putting them through experiences that help generate receptivity to your idea. These things happen unprovably, but faith is part of the excitement of working with God. Without God, you are on your own, implanting and growing that idea in people and resolving the tension you just created in them with your idea. Is it easier with God's help or without?

Tension demands resolution. Resolution, finality, achievement, peace—call it what you like. Resolution is that state that existed before the appealing idea showed up, before we adopted the object of the desire, before we became split.[6] Peace demands that we resolve our divisions.

True, tension is fabulous for moving forward. But we generally hold too many unresolved tensions at the same time. Employee burnout, high employee turnover, fights with unions, the new glitch-laden software rollout that takes a year to fix, being financially overleveraged: so many organizational stresses result from our "I want more" nature and the "we must get to Point B" nature of business. We handle

---

[6] Again, the Hebrew language reflects this reality. In Hebrew, "peace" is "shalom," which comes from "shalem," which means "accounts settled" or "whole." Resolve all debt, and you are at peace. When someone says an intentional goodbye rather than the more casual 'see you later,' they say "shalom," all relationship tension is resolved, all is forgiven, and no one owes anyone anything. Peace. Resolution. Open to what is and what's next.

as much stress individually and organizationally as we can and allow for breakage (people quitting, bad PR) until we implement or drop the intent. Either way, tensions resolve. Consciously adopting common intents through appropriate levels of inclusion in decision making keeps unnecessary intents out and necessary intents implemented.

After resolution, identity. The clarity generated by resolving divisions usually leaves groups with an identity. Trace it backward and you see the identity is the result of the original intent. So, identity is born in Intent. We teach staff to say things such as: "We are _plural noun_ who _exciting and important verb_ to/for _adjective + stakeholder group_." Intently organizing around our intent, it becomes our identity.

Without even blinking, you find yourself saying, "I'm an executive," "I'm a business owner," "I'm a CEO." It's an efficient lie of convenience but a lie nevertheless. Your *identity* is executive, business owner, investor, CEO; you are still *you*. Just think of going home and telling your spouse that their annual bonus depends on them doing the dishes by 8:00.

Too much identity. Our typical relief from the restricted life of an identity is to drop into a different identity. A CEO goes home (or steps out of the home office) and steps into being a spouse, parent, friend, weekend golfer, boater, hunter, wine enthusiast, or philanthropist. However, switching identities brings relief only briefly since *every* identity is solidified purpose (intent). And when intent solidifies into identity, the joy of organic growth gets bogged with the burden of performance. While identity provides us with richness of meaning, it comes at the cost of freedom. Enough identity and we forget how to live free, how to lead with magnanimous, infectious, life-filled, go anywhere do anything power.

When it overtakes your naked sense of self, it is your identity, not you, that creates your experience. You become a vehicle through which identity creates your life. You then believe that your purpose, the imprint you seek to make on the world, *is* your life. When you fuse your life's meaning with your imagined purpose, relationships and the simple enjoyment of the present moment are demoted to secondary meaning. After all, they accomplish nothing unless you use them for your purposes. That is, for the purpose that drives your identity. Welcome to the power of Intent. It's little wonder that organizations hire consultants to train on "work-life balance."

After Identity, God

Intention: being purpose-driven, starting with Why; there are various ways to language intent. We hold the purpose-driven life aloft as a great ideal. Rightly so. Worth, honor, and accomplishment all start in Intent. And yet, professionalism and success are stealing great swaths of territory from one of our other primary sources of nourishment: being deeply seen and still loved and respected in the community, in an *in-person* community. Our professionalism and success drive so many of us into the land of love-less burden. Where is the relief?

The biblical book of Psalms asks and answers this question often. In one song, the psalmist cries out: "I lift up my eyes to the hills. From where does my help come?" Then the answer: "My help comes from the Lord, who made heaven and earth."[7] It is immensely difficult to drop out of identity,

---

[7] Psalm 121:1-2, English Standard Version (ESV)

though it is perhaps a little easier for the very old. For the rest of us to accomplish such a herculean task, we need help from someone beyond all those who have interest in our identity. We need God.

Thus, the 'who you are vs who your identity is' is so grandly important to your relationship with God. If your identity stands in front of God when you call on Him, don't expect Him to be deeply moved. Would God help you achieve your intent if it only strengthens an identity as an executive, owner, or CEO? What are identities to God if *you* are not firmly there as the one who relates with God from your heart of hearts, from your core? God seeks relationships with people who have identities, not with identities that have people.

Suppose you want a powerful relationship with God. In that case, you have to relate to him directly, vulnerably, nakedly, and openly, not seeing yourself as CEO, philanthropist, spouse, person of this or that race or nationality, or whatever. God sees right through your identity. You cannot rely on your identity if you want a power-filled living relationship with God. In front of God, you must stand naked. *That* is an inherent part of *God's* Intent. Without that nakedness, we are still sewing together those metaphorical fig leaves, covering ourselves so that God won't see us in our striving for success without Him.

If you find your identity taking over your prayer, as if God should give your business identity what it wants just because you are taking time to pray, stop. Take a step back to basics. God is the Creator; *you* are His creation. It would be wise to thank Him for everything you can think of until any hidden belief that your identity deserves to win drops away like an overripe grape from the vine. You remain with God. Remaining with God avoids identity solidification.

God, you, and Intent. The first way we reveal our intent is by consistent decision-making. How do you work with God in decision-making? There are two basic ways. Those who want a direct, intimate relationship with God will pray at the appropriate moment, trying to suss out if their intent is, to put it simply, something that makes God happy. Those who see the person-God relationship as being a bit more distant will look to faith-filled friends and/or the Bible to see which of the many teachings, commands, or stories best fits the situation.

However you do it—and we'll go into that more in the following chapters—you want to know what He thinks.[8] You want His take on your intent. There is nothing like receiving God's guidance: vistas open up before you, surety and excitement flood your being, and you get eager to walk the terrain to move toward your destination.

However you seek His take on your intent, do it intentionally, not casually. You understand that God created the Intent space that you access. You have a sense that forming an intention will be impactful and is something special, "holy ground" where intents oblige you—in front of God—to mean what you say. If an intent is true in you and the organization or team, your God-backed intent will generate power and movement.

---

[8] While each of the first six chapters develops the reader's ability to discern the will or voice of God, a good exploration of that would be an entire book in itself. There are many of those available. I strongly recommend Dallas Willard's *Hearing God: developing a conversational relationship with God* (2012, InterVarsity Press).

> **Action Step**
>
> Tell God your intent and ask Him to get involved in it. Listen carefully for depth of truth as you speak to God. The deeper the truth you speak, the clearer the response, which may even appear immediately or in the coming days.

The Three Sources of Intent

It takes work to discern what is authentically *our* intent. Discerning *our* intent is critical for successful implementation; we can't and won't carry others' intents the full distance to successful implementation unless we make them *our* intent.

The three sources of intent available are:

1. Your intent,
2. God's intent, and
3. all the other intents out there.

We just talked about your intent. As the chapters progress, we'll explore God's intent more deeply. This book does not address the third source much; weed out other intents with great gusto. It's good to collaborate, but once the collaborative intent is agreed upon, believe in it and focus upon it. Have faith, see the uncreated future, call on God regularly, loop Him in, and work with hope for and trust in God's guidance. Discern the three sources.

God and Intent

If God calls in an office and we aren't there to hear Him, He does not exist for us at that moment. But regardless of whether we enter that office, God exists and calls out to us. And He has intentions. Intentions even for us. And His intentions are good, worth holding as our 'Point B.' As the ancient prophet Jeremiah said: "I know the thoughts I think about you, declares the Lord, thoughts of peace and not evil, to give you a [good] end and a hope."[9]

The question is: do we engage with faith? Or are we enough in and of ourselves? Maybe our overall intention is to include God, but when we're about to dig that first ceremonial shovel into the ground, do we know to the best of our ability that God is with us in building the building? Your intent should never contradict God's intent. That would be to waste time.

Catch God's Intentions

In my twenties, I remember listening to a cassette tape of Werner Erhard, founder of EST and The Forum. He was giving a talk in DC, and, as was his style, challenged his audience. He said something like this:

> *Go out on the Potomac some winter's night and look up at the stars. Look at the Milky Way. See how bright and beautiful and fabulously awesome the universe is. And ask yourself: "For whom do those stars move?" Don't just ask it, but really mean it, as if your life depends on it, "for whom do those stars move?"*

Long, loud silence. The implication sinks in: the stars—hundreds of billions of massive energy balls burning and

---
[9] Jeremiah 29: 11 (author's translation)

turning in solar systems and galaxies in a celestial distance—those stars absolutely do not turn in the night's sky for you. They don't even know you. Please get some perspective. Get real. He continued:

> *Once you've figured out that they don't move for you, and you stand there in the awe and grandeur of the whole thing and realize the utter insignificance of your desires, maybe, just maybe, you want to get on the side of that for which the stars do move.*

He was talking about getting on the side of truth and honesty. I don't know if he was thinking of God. Maybe. It matters not, for God *is* Truth beyond our divisive factual thinking. But being honest within ourselves is necessary to approach Truth. Whether he was thinking of God or not, Erhard hit the nail on the head: no matter how great our vision, desires, and intentions, they are breathtakingly small in the grand scheme of things. There is something far bigger that can move us when we are moved at all. And all creation knows it. David, the wise and poetic king who built Israel's borders, culture, liturgy, and legacy, said, "The heavens tell of the glory of God, and their expanse declares the work of His hands."[10]

And what's the difference between a galaxy and a leaf to God? Is the God of galaxies not also the Lover of leaves? He sees our intents. The other night, for some reason, I thought to myself: I really want some herring—the pickled kind that comes in a jar with onions. The ones my wife wrinkles her nose at (it's an acquired taste, I'll admit). A minor intent arose

---
[10] Psalm 19:1 (NASB)

in me to get some, but I didn't go to purchase a jar and soon forgot about it. The next morning, my wife stopped at the store and said, "God, what special thing can I get Eliyahu?" He moved her down the aisle and pointed her to the herring. Of course. That's what love does. He would point us to a next career move or get us the right advice on whether to move forward with an IPO. That's what love does. Love loves. Always and forever. It does not matter that our projects are small compared to His. God doesn't lose sight of the forest for the trees and all their leaves. His intention is vast and His implementation is intimate. Stop for a moment and call on Him to guide your eyes as you create your intention. Be a leaf on God's worldwide workplace tree.

Leaves, Trees, Forests, Buildings… What Next?

You might say, "Love is all well and good, but I work remotely a lot. I'm not a leaf, and I hate herring." Fair enough, the poetry part may not be essential. The essential points of this chapter are:

1. Intent is a mode of operation.
2. For effective and efficient operation, create clear intent.
3. For effective and efficient operation, invite God into creating your intent.
4. Eliminate the effect of other intents on your intent.
5. Proceed with faith in yourself and in God.

The next question is: How can we best implement this intent? And the answer is: wisely.

Chapter two

WISDOM

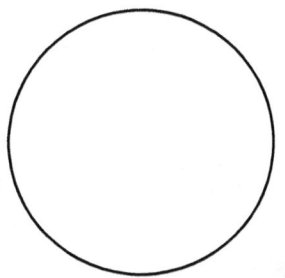

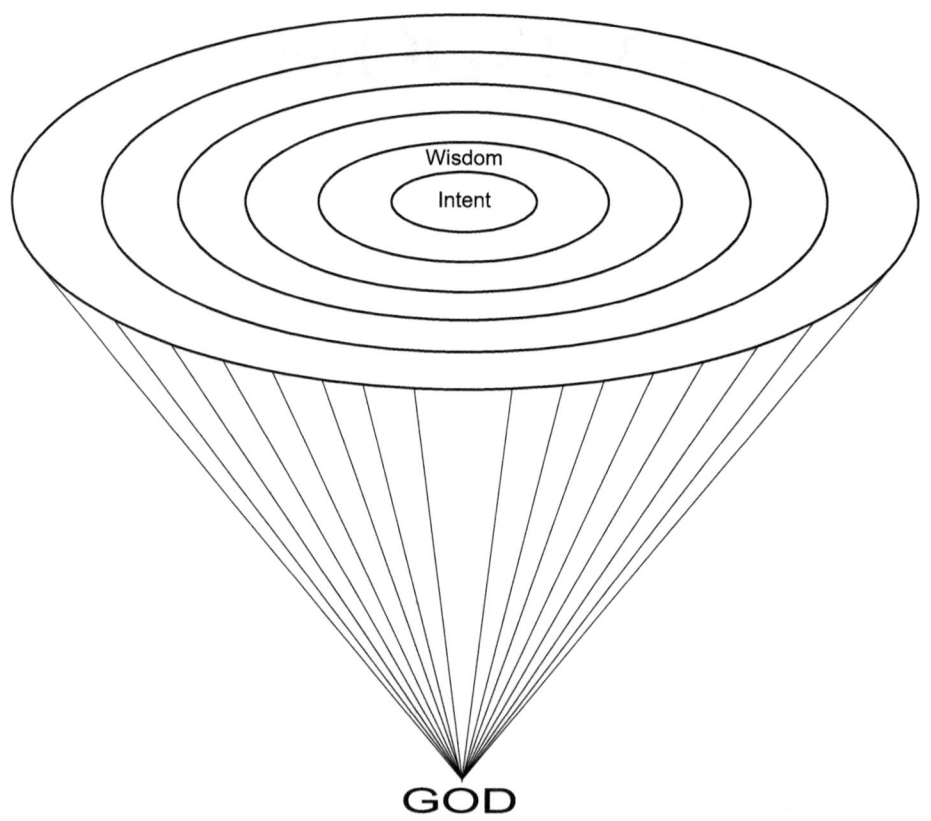

*Therefore do not be unwise, but
understand what the will of the Lord is.*

Ephesians 5:17
(MEV)

You have an intent for a new project, a new program. Okay, now what? Go make it happen. How? Before the shovel in the ground comes the plan on the table. It should be a wise plan.

Show Me the Plan, Stan

Imagine Nike Inc.'s CEO opening its quarterly Senior Leadership meeting by saying, "Okay, everyone, *Just Do It.*" Everyone nods in agreement, the meeting disbands, and they start *just doing it*. At best, that would be utter confusion; at worst, war. Do what, how, when, with whom, for how long, to what end, and to whose benefit? To become real, the vision you took on in Intent needs success criteria tussled over and accepted.

A criterion of vision actualization might be 'achieving the vision without running afoul of the SEC.' Or "add 25% to our bottom line over the next three years by acquisition." The question is, where does the criterion come from, human or heavenly wisdom? *How* you guide the company is as significant to your experience with God as *what* the company is trying to achieve.

If your criteria for success match up with God's criteria, your success will rock. If your success criteria are a product of your desire and habitual thinking, you might succeed in the short term, but in the long term, an "ouch" is waiting for you. Setting the right criteria happens best when you operate in God's mode of Wisdom.

God and Wisdom

What does God have to do with business plans? After all, business is business; God is in the spiritual realm. Even the

Bible says, "The heavens belong to the Lord but the earth He has given to the children of men."[11]

But let me ask you this: as you set out on your endeavor, do you not create your implementation plan and turn to others to see if it makes sense? "Two minds are better than one," as they say. And if one is an infinite mind? And if the infinite mind is loving, caring, and personal enough to want you to succeed? Would you reject such an opportunity and head out on your own? Some of the most famous last words, especially from men, are: "*I got this*."

It is said that "How blessed is the man who fears the Lord."[12] So ask: 'Lord of mine, I'm setting out on this journey, and I don't know whether I know the best way to go about it, but You do. Please grant me wisdom about my journey." Then listen. Listen well. Be alert for incoming information the instant you finish the prayer or even while still praying. You may also need to be patient and let it come upon you down the road. But as soon as you hear, see, feel, or notice something happening in you or in the world around you that you can tell relates to your prayer, thank God for the wisdom and move on it.

For me, wisdom often shows up as a sense of timing. At various junctures in my life, I have had the sense of a powerful window of change in front of me, open for me to walk through. For instance, in my late twenties, my career in photography was taking off. I was in charge of photography for the largest New-Age health center in the country, replete with a studio and a small team of stringers. We provided multiple-use photography, including a magazine with a print circulation of over 100,000 copies. I worked six and a half days a week and loved it.

---
[11]Psalm 115:6 (MEV)
[12]Psalm 112: 1 (NASB1995)

Then, something subtle in my relationship to it changed, and it no longer felt wise to continue. Nothing had changed externally, but I felt my context growing old and lacking meaningful growth. I felt a metaphoric window open up in front of me, and the vista I saw through the window had more of the beckoning of the God I had long ago met than did the vista inside the house. The time had come to start a new life, which I did. And it worked out far better than I could have imagined.

Going with God. If I had weighed the pros and cons, I would not have been accessing wisdom; I would have been using the same criteria of success that I already knew to use. Though I didn't language it this way then, I knew the window was from God. I felt it would be open for a number of months. This may sound abstruse, but wisdom is not analysis. You do not think your way to God's wisdom; you see it inside of you. It is intimate knowing. Human wisdom is the result of much experience in the school of hard knocks; God's wisdom is quietly graced to you. We pause to receive wisdom; otherwise, it comes to us through pain. Pause and receive His wisdom. As it says in the Psalms: "Be still, and know."[13]

> *You do not think your way to God's wisdom; you see it inside of you.*

LEADERSHIP WISDOM: WHAT IT IS AND IS NOT

What it is not. Wisdom is not dictatable. Once, I was part of a not-to-be-named Fortune 100 sales team. We were labeled "Relationship Managers." It's tricky to have a genuine

---

[13] Psalm 46:10 (KJV)

sales relationship, which means mutual respect, give and take, and managing to get as much money as possible from the one with whom you are in relationship. Some of the best salespeople manage it well; I did okay, but it was not my forté.

We Relationship Managers were managed by managers who told us our intent was to meet their revenue quotas. As a condition of employment, that's perfectly fine. But they went further: they also tried to dictate our wisdom. One day, a huge banner appeared in our office, hanging over our heads. One side said:

> A B C

The other side said:

> ALWAYS BE CLOSING

It's understandable that a mid-level manager felt the need to motivate his people, so he tried to get us excited about the only piece that really mattered to him: the close. But because the ABC banner dictated our wisdom to us, it boomeranged. Dictating wisdom to others is counterproductive to generating buy-in. Even when a person buys into someone else's intent, the intent still needs to resonate with their own wisdom. Just ask Ralph.

Ralph was wicked smart, good-hearted, funny, made his numbers, and provided for his family. When we noticed management's "motivational" banner, a general moan went up in the sales cubicles. Ralph looked at the ABC banner and said loudly, "Yup, always be closing; don't do anything else!" He picked up his phone, hit some keys as if to dial, and said: "Hi, Mary? My name is Ralph DeFranco (not his real name) from [name of our company]. Do you want the [expensive data product], or do you want the [really very expensive data product]? Thank you, I'll send the contract. Goodbye." We laughed, and the motivational effort of some well-intended manager was now dead. We knew we were compensated based on our numbers, but it didn't seem wise to Always Be Closing.

What it is. Since then, Netflix and other results-focused companies have redefined managerial wisdom: make sure your reports own your intent but own *their* wisdom. Your what, their how.[14] If they choose right, they win; if they choose wrong, they're gone. David L. Marquet, nuclear submarine commander turned leadership guru, even had his direct reports state their own implementation intent, then he questioned their wisdom. They would adjust their wisdom if he had valid considerations they hadn't included. Then, because his feedback was a contribution to *their* intent, they happily owned a new and improved wisdom, executing on their intent within the larger intent set by Commander Marquet.[15] Setting employee expectations so that they will create their own context within your larger context is the part of organizational wisdom that increases employee engagement and speeds the flow of valuable information and results.

---

[14]Sometimes, they come up with a "what," that is, a task or a project. It is, however, an operational "how" to your vision's "what."

[15]Marquet calls this "Intent-Based Leadership" and describes it in *Turn the Ship Around, Leadership is Language*, and on YouTube.

And yet, that is still only human leadership wisdom; we still need to get to God's leadership wisdom.

Three Sources of Wisdom

In generating wisdom by working with God, be very clear about whose wisdom you are recreating. I recommend categorizing wisdom into three sources:

1. *Your* wisdom,
2. *God's* wisdom, and
3. all the other wisdom out there.

We'll focus on the first two sources. If you agree with another's wisdom, it becomes your own.

Your Wisdom

To work with God as a mature executive, you need to know your own voice and have your own wisdom. There is room for learning of course, but be ready with a store of trustworthy wisdom. That means you decide what the meaningful context is for your intent. And there couldn't be a better example of choosing your own context than Victor Frankl.

Victor's Story

Day after day, Victor Frankl watched the people around him die. Some were shot, some were gassed, some were killed by disease, many starved, and many just gave up the will to live. He understood that his Nazi overlords had complete control over his destiny. Not only could Victor not choose where he went or what he did, but he knew that if a guard just felt like asserting dominance, *regardless* of how Victor behaved, Victor would be shot or beaten to death. In a very real way, he was powerless.

But there was one thing Victor realized: no one can take away his ability to determine how to see things, how to create meaning. Victor Frankl knew how to set his context. When every other action was useless, he still found meaning in setting the context in his own mind. Managing to live through a series of death camps, he maintained freedom by choosing how he framed his moments. This choice isn't just true for Victor: nearly half a century after he wrote *Man's Search for Meaning*, a New York Times survey placed it among the ten most influential books in America.[16] If you do not set your context, it will be set for you. And your context is based on your values.

Bias and the Wisdom Thief

Our choices are usually based on how we see, which is strongly influenced by our values. This "lens bias" can stop us from finding the best wisdom for the situation. To beware of bias, get underneath language to see facts. A simple way to do that is to look at the function a phrase serves for those who use it, then ask yourself if that function supports or thwarts your intent.

Example: The Supermarket and the City. Let's say your intent is to open a grocery store. Where? Scan the world with a question mark, asking, "Does it meet my criteria?" Scanning, you notice a grocery market trend of putting full-scale supermarkets in urban food deserts. 'Urban deserts' and 'food deserts' refer to inner city neighborhoods with

---

[16] https://www.nytimes.com/1991/11/20/books/book-notes-059091.html

small marts and bodegas that mostly sell packaged goods and provide little in the way of cost-effective, life-sustaining nutritious ingredients for home cooking.

High population density without supermarkets can be good candidates for what Harvard Business School Professor and innovation guru Clayton Christensen calls "non-consumption," that is, an untapped market.[17] Super opportunity. But you could have missed it if you saw the opportunity as being in an 'inner city,' which suggests high risk. But people who live there do not call it "the inner city." They simply use their neighborhood name. Our catchphrases lull us into missing the truth and its opportunity.

You, however, stepped out from the hold that *"the inner city"* had on your mind; you saw and paused on the trend of supermarket openings in food deserts. You call some people; you do some research. You discover that most people living in urban food deserts are people just like you, responsible, wanting good health, ready to pay for it, and ready to protect their community resource that provides healthy food to their families and jobs for their children and neighbors. You have now accessed a nonconsumer market. You catch a golden opportunity because you got underneath wording that others used for *their* purposes. You just accessed Wisdom to generate your own wisdom.

Do that with your business. Get under the jargon. Hear the way you speak about your internal motivations and abilities. You don't have to believe your language. See jargon for what it is: a distorter of reality, the reign of other people's wisdom.

---

[17]*Competing Against Luck* (2016); *The Prosperity Paradox: How Innovation Can Lift Nations Out of Poverty* (2019).

> **Action Step**
>
> Describe, in writing, a work problem or opportunity. Replace every piece of jargon with clear and complete language that utilizes 'W's (What, hoW, When, Who, Why, Where). Ask yourself what your language reveals about personal and organizational biases. See if you can't find a potential solution in the rewrite.

God's Wisdom

Knowing God's wisdom about any particular situation is an iffy proposition, so many of us don't try. But the grandness and perfection of God's wisdom should entice us, no? After all, for whom do the stars move? Not for me, not for my wisdom, not for you, not for your wisdom. Even if we are Socrates, Solomon, or Morgan Freeman, the stars move for God, and we should too.

But how?

Two Ways to Get God's Wisdom

There are two major ways to access God's wisdom:

1. Ask God to drop it into your life, then watch and listen for it to show up. It could show up any place, any time. Perhaps the diner waitress will say something that echoes in your head, and you got it. It wasn't the diner waitress speaking; it was God. Or it just pops into your mind quietly, so be sure to catch the pearl.
2. Ask God to show it to you in the Bible, then start reading. Read slowly. If something doesn't make sense, think about it. Maybe talk it over with someone who has really studied the Bible. Then, go

back and read again. Keep reading. At some point, something jumps out of the book and settles your perspective.

For example, your CHRO proposes a leadership development program (LDP) for the whole senior leadership. It would be a good thing for the team, but at the moment everyone is at maximum capacity. You battle between long term benefit and short term doability. You pray for wisdom. You believe that God heard you but so far no 'aha' moment. You pick up the Bible and find this little speech:

"Why do you look at the speck of sawdust in your brother's eye and pay no attention to the plank in your own eye? How can you say to your brother, 'Let me take the speck out of your eye,' when all the time there is a plank in your own eye? You hypocrite, first take the plank out of your own eye, and then you will see clearly to remove the speck from your brother's eye."[18]

Because you prayed for wisdom before reading, the words of Jesus' short speech might have lit up with relevance to your decision. Or maybe not; maybe you have a vague feeling that there is a message in this for the situation, but you don't discern it clearly.

You ponder it. The message from God here seems to be that people should take full and honest responsibility for themselves and their people before pointing out the negative consequences of actions (or inactions) of other executives and

---
[18] Matthew 7:3-5 (NIV)

their people. But does that mean that God is actually telling you it's a wise idea to do the training, or is He just showing you that your team's responsibility level is more of a problem than you thought? Analysis may not answer the question.

To understand God's wisdom, that is, the context He is trying to focus you on, you metaphorically turn your eyes again towards God, asking again for wisdom about what this plank and dust stuff means to whether it's a good idea to do the LDP. You believe that God is providing you with wisdom. After all, God's Spirit brought order out of the deep and dark ambiguity of the situation in Genesis 1:2 ("and the earth was formless and void"); He can structure and clarify this hazy choice too. So you head towards God. You re-ask and re-listen with ready willingness to act on God's message of wisdom. This time, behold, insight appears. The process is not mysterious, it is simply connecting with God in Wisdom mode.

You envision a change to the structure of your executive team meetings. Now each person who reports not meeting a goal will state what the plank in their own eye (fear or selfish motive) has been when they look at this goal. And everyone who reports being on track to meet a goal can volunteer to state what they could do better for the whole team and organization if they would not let _name of selfish or indulgent motive_ influence _name of specific decision_. Everyone agrees that if they can't see their plank, the others will question them from the point of view of their own insight, which may of course be influenced by their own different needs and interests. Tough love perhaps, but it is more effective than a 90-minute presentation and more efficient than a full-day leadership development training. This solution came because you used prayer and some Bible reading to connect with God in Wisdom.

Chapter Three

IMPETUS

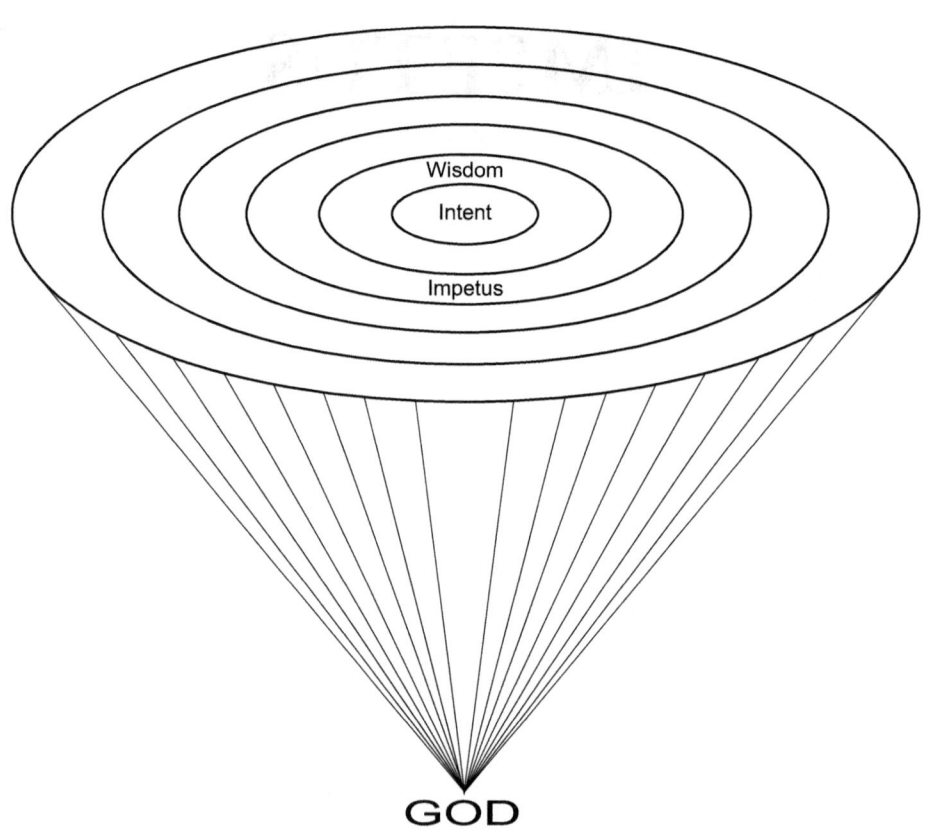

Thirty seconds and counting. Astronauts report it feels good. T-25 seconds. Twenty seconds and counting. T-15 seconds, guidance is internal. 12, 11, 10, 9 ... ignition sequence start ... 6, 5, 4, 3, 2, 1, 0 ... All engines running. Liftoff! We have a liftoff.

NASA Mission Control, Apollo 11

In Intent, you said, "I want this to happen." In Wisdom, you said, "This is how it should happen." Step into Impetus, and it happens; your intent moves from thought to thing, and your commitment isn't just words anymore; it is now using resources.

If you start a company from scratch, it's easy to feel when you enter Impetus. There is that revolutionary moment when an organization bursts forth into a new "is." That moment happens in Impetus. Most change comes from evolving circumstances and systems. Companies typically reorganize themselves at the subsystem level, a bit at a time. Business units or departments create new programs or projects. Regardless of scale, beginnings and 90° turns demand impetus.

Kimberly-Clark's Story

In *Good to Great,* Jim Collins brings a good example of Impetus in the middle of ongoing operations. Kimberly-Clark's CEO in the 1970s and 80s, Darwin Smith, recognized that the market was slowly changing around them and decided to sell the paper mills that had forever been the bedrock of their vertically integrated business. He raised a billion dollars by selling their paper mills. Kimberly-Clark had to succeed in its chosen market. They moved fully to compete in the paper goods space, challenged and overcame even Proctor & Gamble. Had Smith not entered Impetus, they would have hung on to the mills and not had the cash to acquire the companies it needed to top the paper consumer goods space. They would have died a slow death.

Defining Impetus

The Impetus mode is God's spiritual structure that best supports transforming intent into existence and idea into fact. Like most spiritual things, a "spiritual structure" is challenging to define. To some it feels like a stage along the way, a season; to others it is like "the zone" where things click into place. Impetus is a space in which you meet the power that God has available for you, a power you'll need to harness in the next three operational modes. Like the other modes, it's a meeting place for God and the world, where God moves in the specifics of who, what, when, where, and why. But Impetus is a unique space where ideas coalesce into reality.

When God created the world, He moved through six days of Impetus, in which each day, He transformed word to world, thought to thing. Although God is resting beyond creation, we are still here working in the sixth day, and He is also with us. God touches the world; we meet Him and transform.

Inside us, impetus is an emotional imperative that uses power to coalesce ideas into action.

Impetus: Passion and Focus

In Impetus, we access two of God's great gifts: passion and focus. Passion is fire and determination. Focus controls that fire. Enlivened by passion, intent and wisdom solidify into a clear imperative.

> *Impetus is your emotional imperative.*

A "plane" at the gate is a "flight" only in our thoughts. Right now, it's just a plane with an intent (and hopefully wisdom) attached. To move from thought to thing, the plane enters Impetus with the okay from the tower to take off. Its engines ignite, its brakes release, and it takes flight. Projects, partnerships, processes, and products all start with a thought. To be a business, they move past thought and into the efforts to get them launched. The disparate actions necessary for launch come together in a burst of unified, focused propulsion, and the business launches.

In our flight example, in Impetus, passengers converge at the airport, funnel past vendors on their way to the plane, the ground crew fills fuel tanks and conducts a host of other preparations, and the plane taxis the runway and takes off.

Once the plane levels off a bit and settles into flight, the reality of the runway is gone; a flight is born. The service is being delivered, moving customers from A to B. The airline delivers value and earns its reward. Impetus facilitated that transition from the idea of flight to the reality of flight.

In actualizing value, business gets real. You shift what you see, what you need, what is urgent, and with whom you interact. You reorder priorities. You jettison unproductive ideas and use of resources. You focus resources to provide a service. Now, a problem for one will be a problem for all unless you deal with it. A success for one is a success for all. In this way, bit by quick bit, your commitments manifest.

Action Step

Ask yourself: *Does my intent have sufficient passion and focus to take the right people to a new reality? If not, who and/or what needs to change?*

How It Works: The Five Stages of Impetus

If you are a business owner, CEO, executive, or aspiring executive, you have a natural penchant for Impetus. But how does it work? Impetus happens in five stages. If one of your projects is not gaining traction, look to see which of the five stages needs help. The stages are:

1. Focus
2. Propulsion
3. Movement
4. Momentum
5. Takeoff

In **Focus**, you see your intent only through your front windshield. Distractions are eliminated. Everyone is all in. You make it meaningful by acquiring resources. An example resource is a signed bank loan. Another is dedicated staff. You see how to bring the resources together in perfect timing. You stay focused to harness them and move them forward as one.

Propulsion applies emotion to intent. Emotion propels you to get results and therefore demands that you risk your capital—financial capital, political capital, social capital, intellectual capital, whatever is necessary. When you use capital to acquire resources, your word, name, self-worth, and financial future are at risk, and that propels you to take further action. You are modeling the way; others do as you do. The propulsion of focused passion generates movement.

Movement is created by using your resources. You used the money from the bank loan and the people to build the software; now, you have a product. People respond not only to the product you say you want to provide, but also to what you now can provide. Relationships move your idea into reality. You apply more resources, add propulsion, and make more movement until you generate momentum.

Momentum grows as you tie little movements together into a flow of focused activity. Not only do you accelerate because you feel propelled, but your external commitments pull you out to action. By now, you'd have to push back to stop it.

Takeoff happens when you provide the first service, get your first bid, and get the final project approval and resource allocation. It is also simply when you realize that your business has started, your program is a go, and that this plane is flying on its own, carrying you and your stakeholders to Point B.

Impetus Demands Honesty

Paradoxically, the important question for launch is whether you are grounded enough. Are you serious enough to make that real, actually actual commitment to your new journey? Not the New Year's resolution kind of commitment with a hidden "if I can" in there. In Impetus, you do it or drop it. Once the plane is in the air, returning fuel to the engines is not an option. You get serious fast.

These questions may help you see if you and your idea are sufficiently grounded:

- Do I love this idea enough?
- What am I willing to lose to see it succeed?
- Am I ready to ignite my fuel now?
- If I am still waiting to ignite, for what or whom will I burn?

These are not rhetorical questions. Go ahead, ask yourself those questions. If you don't have enough impetus for your idea to take off, go back into Intent and see what desire rules you really. Not in theory, not ideally, but really.

Impetus is Readily Available

When you are ready to ignite, impetus is readily available. God filled the universe with impetus. It's not just that He *can* make it available to you; He already has. The following examples from Impetus may help you notice it in and around you. What you measure matters, so keep noticing impetus.

Example 1: Driving. My grandparents lived above their dry-goods store in Newark, NJ. Grampa Morris had been driving since the 1920s, first in a Model-T truck, then in other vehicles, and then, by the 1960s, in a sleek and speedy Dodge Dart. As unbelievable as it sounds to us now, he never drove faster than 40 mph. But for most of his driving life, interstates didn't exist. His family, vendors, and the customers to whom he delivered were all nearby. For Grampa, 25 mph was good; 35 was fast. He accessed impetus sufficient for his intent and his context. He added value to people's lives at precisely the right speed. He was kind; delivering mercy, goodness, and groceries as his value add. 25 mph made perfect sense for that.

The moral of the example: Match your propulsion to the nature of your intent and the demands of your wisdom. God does not dislike power if it is for His layered purposes; in fact, He provides the perfect amount.

Example 2: Flying. At the time of this writing, the longest regularly scheduled non-stop commercial flight is about 9,500 miles. It takes 18+ hours.[19] Most travelers do not want to endure such a flight. Nevertheless, Qantas Airlines managed a successful test flight to push the maximum distance to over 11,000 miles and 19+ hours.[20] The flight puts you through two sunrises in the same "day" and completely messes with your sense of time and space. The momentum to launch a successful venture or break a record sometimes needs to be so strong as to mess with people's sense of normal.

The moral of the example: to go beyond, openly invite Impetus, and blow past normal.

Example 3: Space Travel. Soon after Grampa Morris gave up the Dart in 1968, three adventurers rocketed themselves beyond normal and took the whole human race with them. Aldrin, Armstrong, and Collins, intent on walking the moon, risked everything. When their engines ignited, seven and a half million pounds of thrust[21] propelled three men at seven miles per second through the atmosphere, into the nothingness of space, and to another celestial body. With them, all of humanity entered a new reality. The sky was no longer the limit.

---

[19] Porter, S., BBC News. *The World's Longest Non-Stop Flight Takes Off from Singapore.* (10.12.2018). https://www.bbc.com/news/business-45795573
[20] Quest, R., & Neild, B., CNN. *London to Sydney Flight Breaks World Record.* (11.15.2019) https://www.cnn.com/travel/article/qantas-test-flight-london-sydney-nonstop/index.html
[21] http://www.onegiantleap.org/facts.html#ansH. One pound of thrust is the force it takes to prevent one pound from being moved by gravity.

That took a whole lot of focus and emotional imperative. Three astronauts needed NASA and its mental, emotional, logistical, and financial resources That, in turn, required national social-political resources. To provide those 7,500,000 pounds of thrust, they shared Intent and Wisdom with about 400,000 people in 20,000 companies, with the U.S. military, and Presidents Kennedy, Johnson, and Nixon. They lassoed the American people, $24 billion,[22] and the Russian space effort as a foil against which to compete. Aldrin, Armstrong, and Collins found copious impetus.

The moral of the example: there is massive Impetus spread all around. Accessing and focusing it depends on how much and/or how many people want the intent behind the impetus.

Accessing Impetus: One Strategy, Four Tactics

To increase impetus, your strategy is to reduce drag on structure, processes, and team members. You might also find drag in yourself. After all, raise the stakes high enough, and anyone hesitates. Here are four tactics to reduce drag.

Tactic #1: Drop others' intents. Understanding stakeholder needs is important, but one can try to please others too much, drawing impetus away from one's own intent. If you're a servant leader, great, but balance both parts of that moniker. Your best service sometimes is leading.

---

[22]Christianson, S., *Smithsonian Magazine*. *How NASA's Flight Plan Described the Apollo 11 Moon Landing*. https://www.smithsonianmag.com/us-history/apollo-11-flight-plan-180957225/

Tactic #2: Drop negativity. Check team members' internal motivation to see if they operate out of fear, uncertainty, or doubt. FUD points them in two directions at once: forward but wait, no, backward, or maybe... *That* dissolves impetus.

Tactic #3: Choose your new impetus. Letting go of the past frees up energy. Making a clear choice brings together all the energies spent in FUD, nostalgia, and the safety of what you know. Choose or lose.

Choose from any of three sources:

- Logical choice
- Emotional choice
- Knowing

Logical Choice: what *should be*. We look at a situation, see a problem, and decide what to do to solve the problem. There is something so logical about logic; it is a self-evident good thing that we release impetus by making a decision. Logic is also necessary to convince others to get on board, so it helps build impetus. "You should invest in us because... (market analysis)." Logic propels intent.

Emotional Choice: what we *want*. We see a problem and hook into an aversion to pain, and/or we see an opportunity and hook into a desire for satisfaction. Passion is fabulous and also short-sighted. Before making a decision from emotion, run it through someone else's wisdom. If it still seems like the right choice, engage all the passion you have. Release charisma.

Knowing: what *is*. Knowing is not thinking, understanding, or believing. Knowing is being so intimate with content and context that there is no question. The most powerful of the three sources is also the most open to myopic bias and self-deception. To name just a few biases: gender bias, racial bias, recency bias, confirmation bias (using evidence to confirm pre-existing belief), and height bias (American CEOs are on average 3 inches taller than other employees). But regardless of the danger of bias, sometimes you must go with your gut. It gives you impetus, endurance, and results. And risk. But there you are: Impetus is a risky and exhilarating place to be.

Tactic #4: Drop selfishness. Selfishness is focusing one's concerns inward. People don't share their resources with selfish people unless they are manipulated into doing it. And if you are busy being concerned about yourself, God sees that you don't want His help, so He doesn't intervene on your behalf either.

God's Impetus

Q: Why even seek God's impetus when you already have access to it? A: Sometimes, the mountains are just too high to climb without some extra oxygen. God is the source and unending font of hyper-oxygenated impetus. And He likes to help. So why not ask? Jesus succinctly said, "Ask and it will be given to you."[23]

God can always give you the perfect amount of perfectly timed propulsion to move you the perfect distance. God's propulsion may come from anywhere. It could be money from an as-yet-untrusted source. It could be an experience offered to you that is not on your list of good ways to use your time but ends up motivating you.

---

[23] Matthew 7:7 (ESV)

> *Aim for the highest: do it with God.*

Trust. Invite God into your business. You can trust that He will enter in a kind way, a way that can work. If your level of impetus needs to be like Grampa's 35 mph Dodge Dart, then He will provide that; if it needs to be 25,000 mph to get to the moon, mars, or beyond, then that's what He'll arrange for you. God is powerful, precise, and perfect.

Prodding. In an intimate relationship with God, God will prod you when you aren't honest with yourself. He'll use your conscience so you can see and be free of lies. It's an excellent idea to stop and listen and to listen and stop. He'll use your investors, your spouse, reports, random people on the street, anything, and anyone at any time. He may even talk to you directly, audibly, anything to keep pushing you to your deepest level of truth. *If*, that is, you sincerely give Him permission. If you give Him permission to propel your organization to a new reality, He will provide the circumstances that will prompt you to jettison that which slows momentum.

Just ask Him, or plead if you are passionate: "God, please move me. Move my organization." Then, do your best not to stop Him when He challenges the status quo that you just asked Him to help change. Remember, sometimes the change He points out has to start with you.

A note of caution. If you sense that you are pushing yourself, your family, your partners, or your project too hard to reach the goal, you might have hit the sand trap of pride and its hidden counterpart, fear. It is so easy for pride to enter through a "whatever it takes" commitment. If you sense that pursuing your intent is not aligned with God's will, no matter how much pressure to implement, don't do it; back out. Otherwise, He might let you get what you ask for; and with it, the consequences. In real life, that means pain. To reveal whether you are using too much push, answer this question honestly:

> **Action Step**
>
> *In this project/plan/person/area/action, are you most motivated by fear for self or by love for God?*
>
> *Wherever you are motivated by fear for yourself, bring the fear to God in prayer and tell Him you are fearful. Give the fear to Him. If you can find it deep enough inside you, give your need to hold on to fear to God. Remember God's inviolable goodness and reassert your trust in His guidance for you and the organization in your care. If you take God's protection, you will survive and be the better for it.*

Impetus is the space where God unites so many moments to propel you forward. It can seem like high stakes. But you will end up in a whole other future when you let go of whatever fear or pride it is that holds you back or derails you. Then, with God's wind (spirit) at your back, you really get going.

Chapter Four

GO

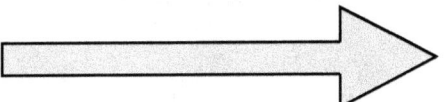

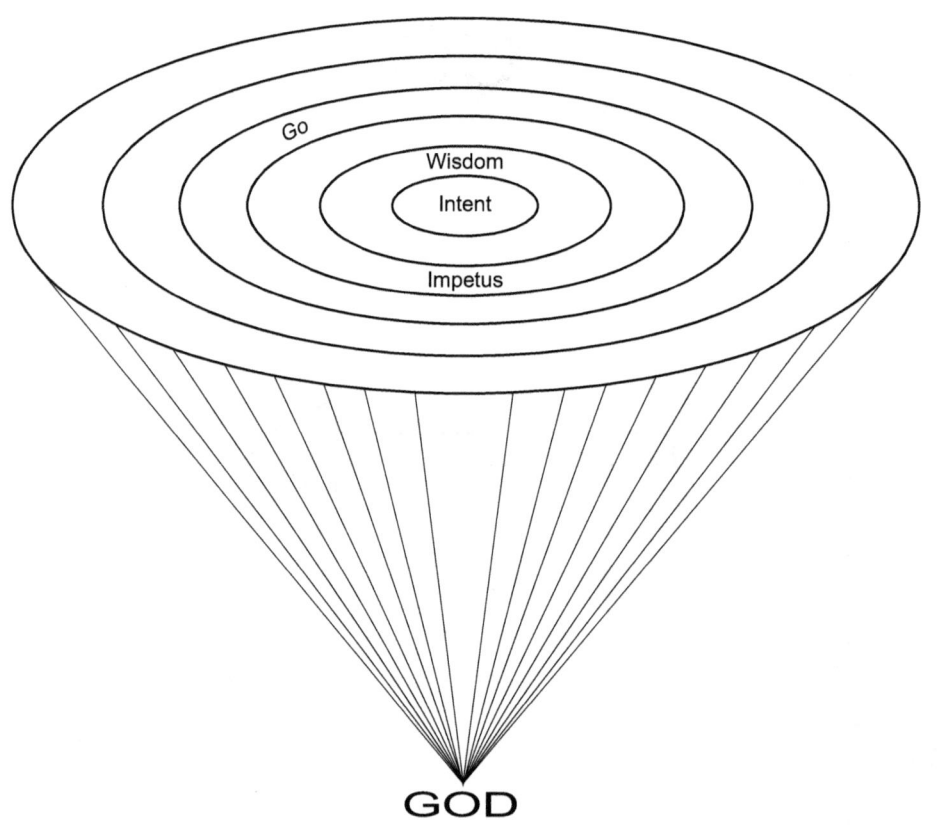

"Now the Lord said to Abram, 'Walk yourself out of your land, out of your birthplace, out of your father's house, to a land that I will show you…' **And Abram walked."**

Genesis 12:1, 4
Author's translation and bolding

You have your intent. In Wisdom, you gave it guidance. Exploding onto the scene through Impetus, you land in "*Go*" mode and deliver intent. You committed to specific deliverables within a specific timeframe to investors, staff, clients, vendors, and other stakeholders. Now, do it. Deliver on your commitments.

Go is the mode God uses to keep us moving. All we want to do when we are in it is get things done. Its key quality is forward motion. Aware of tick-tocking time, we are *get-it-done* fireballs. And we love it. Sell it, make it, deliver it, and receive our reward. "Pass GO and collect $200." "Just do it." *Go* manifests action; when focused, productivity. Perform, deliver, repeat. In a way, *Go* is the archetypical American mode. We are practical people committed to (some might say addicted to) doing. "Git 'er done."

> **Go** *is "do" mode: perform & produce.*
> **Go** *changes reality.*

In a project's early stages, we access *Go* and likely get one thing done at a time, sequentially. In a project's mid and late stages, or an organization's mid-lifecycle stages, we get multiple things done simultaneously. Either way, *Go* is the mode through which God has us deliver on intent. *Go* seems to be the mode in which value is actually created. However, it creates a specific value that it makes in specific places for specific people, as guided by other modes.

Impetus is explosive. *Go* is fast-paced but grounded and steady rather than explosive. Where Impetus was your mode for a starburst of sudden change, *Go* is the space where—by God's grace and our efforts—you establish that reality as you daily produce and reproduce your services and products. You make stuff (product) and/or make stuff happen (service). You build brand. You generate revenue. You win market share. "You *Go, girl!*"

And, *Go* God. Before starting your breathless day, remember to pray. This is the time for short, simple, but sincere prayer. Thank God for the wonderous possibilities in the day ahead of you. Then, Ask God for strength to keep doing, the wisdom to stay focused on intent, and to remember Him so you two can partner. Remember that without Him, nothing works. You might be the engine in this partnership, but God is the steering wheel and the master map maker.

You do the do, and God smiles. You do an Abram: you walk yourself out of the home of your old vision into a greater land. Maybe God didn't literally command you to take a walk, but you took steps in the direction of God's desire and are now in greater territory. As Jesus's brother James wrote, "faith by itself, if it has no works, is dead."[24] Faith alone, the kind you needed to sustain you through Intent, is an almost, not a cigar. In *Go*, you make cigars. So *Go* ahead, light up.

GO DEFINED

The mode of *Go* is the spiritual space where your organization produces the value for which customers and funders pay. By "spiritual space," I don't mean a church, nor do I mean a reverent or other-worldly state of mind. God is full of life and

---
[24]James 2: 17 (NRSV)

is there where we engage: in the office, through emails, phone calls, and Zoom.

Go in organizations is God's subtle structure to promote thoughts, feelings, desires, surroundings, and purposes that contribute to getting stuff done. Though the quantity and quality of your organization's *Go* is filtered through your structures, processes, people, and culture, *Go* shows up as activity and creates *more*.

Mark's Story

God gifted Mark Whitacre with brains and energy. As a young man, he earned a Ph.D. in biochemistry from Cornell and quickly rose into corporate leadership. Back in the 1980s, career advancement still meant years of climb. But not for gifted Mark. By the time he was 32, he was president of a division of Archer Daniels Midland (ADM), a large global food processing corporation. At 35, he was a corporate VP and likely successor to ADM's president. Clearly, Mark was full of *Go*. Decades later, he still is; that's one of the amazing things about him.

Go-ing, he achieved results: a 13,000 sq ft home, seven fine automobiles, a stable of horses, and people who would walk by and look with admiration (or envy) at the man who could do this. His intent was status; his method was achievement. With clear intent and bursting with impetus, he went directly to *Go* (and kept collecting $200). We'll hear more of Mark's story later, but for now, Mark is *Go*-ing.

Go in Your Organization

You can find *Go*, for instance, in the liveliness of a business unit or department. How does the unit relate to progress, to creating, adding, and expanding? To getting out there and interacting with the public? How does it relate to speed? Not just in theory or talk, but in actuality: does it produce? Does it continually produce more than before?

Go departments, Go functions. If it's a "measure four times before cutting" kind of department, it's not *Go*. However, if the function of a department is to acquire, produce, build, create, make noise, catalyze change, or get stakeholders their stuff, it is in *Go*. *Go* units push; *Go* units expect it done yesterday. They care more about reward than about risk. They are outward-focused, change-oriented, impassioned teams of inspirational forward motion. They make things happen and get people clappin'.

> *Remember: Nothing Goes without God.*

Here are examples of what are typically *Go* functions:

- Acquisitions (M&A)
- Business Development
- Community Outreach
- Customer Service
- Employee Development
- Fundraising
- Government Relations
- Investing
- Logistics, Distribution
- Marketing
- Product Research & Development

- Production
- Public Relations
- Sales

Hold this list loosely; add or subtract to it. Your Accounts Receivable, for instance, might have a mission to empower delinquents to generate their own income. They spend hours on the phone understanding client needs, researching solutions for them, and reaching back out to teach them financial literacy or help them create a new income stream. That kind of AR would operate in *Go* because its focus is changing the external environment rather than conserving a particular cash-to-asset ratio for the company. Similarly, a unit that is not characteristically a *Go* unit (think Accounting) can be in *Go* mode for a time (think tight IRS audit deadline).

Note that *Go* mode isn't about innovation per se. To innovate, you need all of the first six modes. The innovator's uniqueness sits in Intent: the new idea, vision, and way of seeing. *Go* departments are producers; they get the innovation out there.

Go structure, Go process. There is no single rule about how *Go* structures and processes should be designed. They can centralize or diffuse authority. By way of example, many HR processes are designed to prevent negative outcomes to organizational safety and stability. Since HR often functions to avoid the risk of litigation and maintain employee satisfaction, it is not a *Go* function. However, in small and medium-sized organizations, training and employee development are often placed in HR. They are *Go* functions, making "HR-D" a *Go* function, and giving HR Directors split priorities. HR maintains; HR-D develops.

In a *Go* unit, an idea can't have to move through layers of people who can say "no" before it finds the one who can say "yes." Hence, skipping processes while intoning the *Go* motto—better to ask forgiveness than permission—is more likely to happen in a *Go* department. If you are a process person, forgive them; they're just trying to do their job. Their idea of a good process is the shortest route from A to B. Have them read the next chapter, No, to grow a fuller understanding of the value of the process.

Go culture. A *Go* department or project needs a *Go* culture to support its *Go* function, structure and processes. Its indoor climate buzzes with action, bright lights, and whiteboards. Its online climate is dynamic with popups and interactive platforms. *Go* culture promotes people quickly.

Go organizations ask by how many points they can beat the Dow Jones average this month or what company they can acquire next. Its environment is impatience. Ad-hoc teams form, do things, break up, move on. *Go* culture is action-oriented and has a guiding norm of "get it done, whatever it takes." Norms, SOPs, and aspirational values that appear on the company website and press releases rely on words such as "new," "dynamic," "cutting edge," "capture," "increase," and "more."

Go operates with hidden assumptions. For instance, the organization might hold the unstated belief that there is no such thing as a free lunch. They enshrine the value of hard work and build productivity into compensation. It may also believe that people are naturally good, and create a CSR department to go give back to the community. In *Go*, beliefs generate action. Ten-hour days are nothing noteworthy.

***Go* employees.** *Go* people are "on the go," task-oriented, born with a cup of coffee in one hand and a to-do list in the other. Hopefully, your *Go* people also have the emotional intelligence not to sweat the small stuff. That way, they turn and keep going when *their* idea or method doesn't happen. They maintain forward motion. A highly capable *Go* person will also have the EQ to get others *Going*. They have *Go* careers and are called rising stars, rock stars, superstars, and hi-pos.

***Go* in organizational lifecycle.** Now that we see what, where, and who *Go* is, there is the how much and when of *Go*. How much *Go* is appropriate is, in part, a function of industry. It would be inappropriate for a savings and loan to be structured and cultured for as much *Go* as a pizza shop.

How much *Go* is appropriate for your business is also a function of its place on the organizational lifecycle. To see how the modes of *Go* and the next two modes—No and Prime—relate to the organizational lifecycle, we'll use a simplified four-phase model:

1. **Ideation & Formation:** Dreaming, thinking, talking, and planning; making it legal; telling the world.
2. **Production:** Focus on sales, production, and service delivery; effectiveness over efficiency; focus on revenue first, profit second; need for more cash.
3. **Apex:** Inclusive attention to structure, processes, *and* people; effectiveness *and* efficiency, short *and* long term. Investing surplus revenue for stable growth. Order supplants chaos, and compliance is valued.
4. **Hardening of the Arteries:** Structure and process are set (in concrete). Stability wins, passion loses, innovation dies. Acquire other businesses whose blood still

flows fast and free, then manage revenue. Nonprofits reach the limits of their mission effectiveness and become less relevant.

Differentiating modes from phases. In each lifecycle phase, the organization will likely access some modes more than others. In phase 1 of the organizational lifecycle, Ideation & Formation, the first triad of modes (Intent, Wisdom, and Impetus) are most needed and most accessed, but not exclusively. In lifecycle phases 2 and 3, the Production and Apex phases, the second triad of modes (*Go*, *No*, and *Prime*) are more needed and accessed. In Hardening of the Arteries, the mode of No is the default mode, outweighing the action of *Go* or the sensible agility of Prime. Each phase draws more on some modes than others, but all modes are accessed across the lifecycle to varying degrees.

In Production, you are all about *Go*. If you fret that it's too chaotic, that's normal. In Hardening of the Arteries, you are all about No. More on No in the next chapter, but suffice it to say that you need to reinject *Go* here. To reinvigorate the organization (or program, project, or person) with *Go*, you would likely need an overall organizational self-re-examination through the first three *modes*—Intent, Wisdom, and Impetus. Course correction is normal. The key is to keep *Go* alive by interacting openly with new circumstances. One thing is clear: if there is no *Go*, the company is a no-go.

Organizational Action Step

Take the time to look at whether your organization (or unit, department, team, or project) is well set for the appropriate amount of *Go*. Consider:

- location in the lifecycle,
- current strategic objectives
- short-term tactical needs.

Optimize the following for *Go*:

- structures,
- processes,
- culture, including inter-unit communications, and
- key team members.

> *Go is the primary mode accessed in the second phase of the organizational lifecycle.*

GO AND GOD

God loves *Go*. More accurately, God loves for <u>us</u> to be in *Go*. The Bible starts with Impetus as God puts out words that manifest our physical reality from nothing.[25] God didn't actually go anywhere or do anything. He willed (Intent) and spoke (Wisdom), and the result was creation (Impetus). Then, His first instruction to us was to take the material that He had created and do stuff with it. He tells us to use the material at hand to manufacture more.[26]

---

[25] "In the beginning, God created heaven and earth. The earth was formless and void... God said, 'Let there be light,' and there was light." (Gen 1:1-3 ESV)

[26] "So God created man and... said to them, 'Be fruitful and multiply.'" (Gen 1:27-28 ESV)

Go with God

So, let's get to work making more. How do you *Go* with God? First things first: as leadership gurus Kouzes & Posner say, you have to "model the way."[27] If you don't *Go* with God, your organization probably won't either. So, how? By bringing your theories, practical experience, and skill to the situation.

God, *Go*, You, and Prayer. If your own experience of God includes prayer, pray. If it doesn't, give prayer a go anyway. Reveal your thoughts but also your heart. Ask in truth. Quiet, gentle, and intimate, He hears. Ask God to guide you. Even ask for specific instructions about if to go, when to go, how to go, how far to go with a project, with whom to go, etc. Listen, watch, feel, wait; you may hear, see, understand. In answering your prayer, God can add His wisdom to your doing.

The prayer approach can be challenging: it is entering the subjective. Leaders are expected to be objective; all of science backs objectivity and getting it right. Objective facts explain failures and blunt criticism. Add a mode of subjectivity, e.g., I *think* God is indicating to do this, and you add a mode of risk. But there you are. This book is for executives and entrepreneurs. *Go* sometimes demands more emotional and spiritual courage than we want to use. But in the end, No guts? No glory.

Remember, God is always here with you. And God is good. And He renews your ability to go on. Let's take two examples from the Bible, where God renewed strength in the extreme.

---

[27]Kouzes, James M., and Barry Z. Posner. 2017. *The Leadership Challenge*. 6th ed. New York, NY: John Wiley & Sons.

2nd Kings:

When Elisha entered the house, behold the boy was dead, laid out on his bed. So he entered and shut the door behind them and prayed to the Lord. Then... the flesh of the child became warm... then the boy opened his eyes. [28]

Not only is God alive but in *Go*, He responds to prayer by breathing life into dead people, mortally wounded teams, and ailing organizational units. Imagine the increased life He can put into your *healthy* employees, teams, and projects. Are you praying to God about your *Go* teams' aliveness?

Gospel of John:

Now in Jerusalem by the Sheep Gate there is a pool, which in Hebrew is called Bethesda, having five porches. In these lay a great crowd of invalids, blind, lame, and paralyzed, waiting for the moving of the water... After the stirring of the water, whoever stepped in first was healed of whatever disease he had. A certain man was there who had an illness for thirty-eight years.

When Jesus saw him lying there, and knew that he had been in that condition for a long time, He said to him, "Do you want to be healed?" The sick man answered Him, "Sir, I have no one to put me into the pool when the water is stirred. But while I am coming, another steps down before me."

Jesus said to him, "Rise, take up your bed and walk." Immediately the man was healed, took up his

---

[28] 2 Kings 4: 32-35 (NASB)

bed and walked… Jesus said to them, "My Father is working still, and I am working."[29]

In the second example, the person was so stuck that he didn't even say "Yes" to the offer of being able to move again. In any case, God heard his heart.

Individuals, teams, and companies all get paralyzed in various ways to various degrees at various times. But God's love can move us. Whatever the lifecycle stage, department, or situational challenge, you are in *Go* if you seek God to get going. Just remember, He may allow you to "rise, take up your bed and walk," that is, leave your current way of seeing and doing things and walk on in a new way. Be able and willing to go. But you may also discover that He is not giving you that miracle to move forward because you *should not* go forward, at least not in that direction at that time.

---

[29]John 5: 2-17 (MEV)

Chapter Five

NO

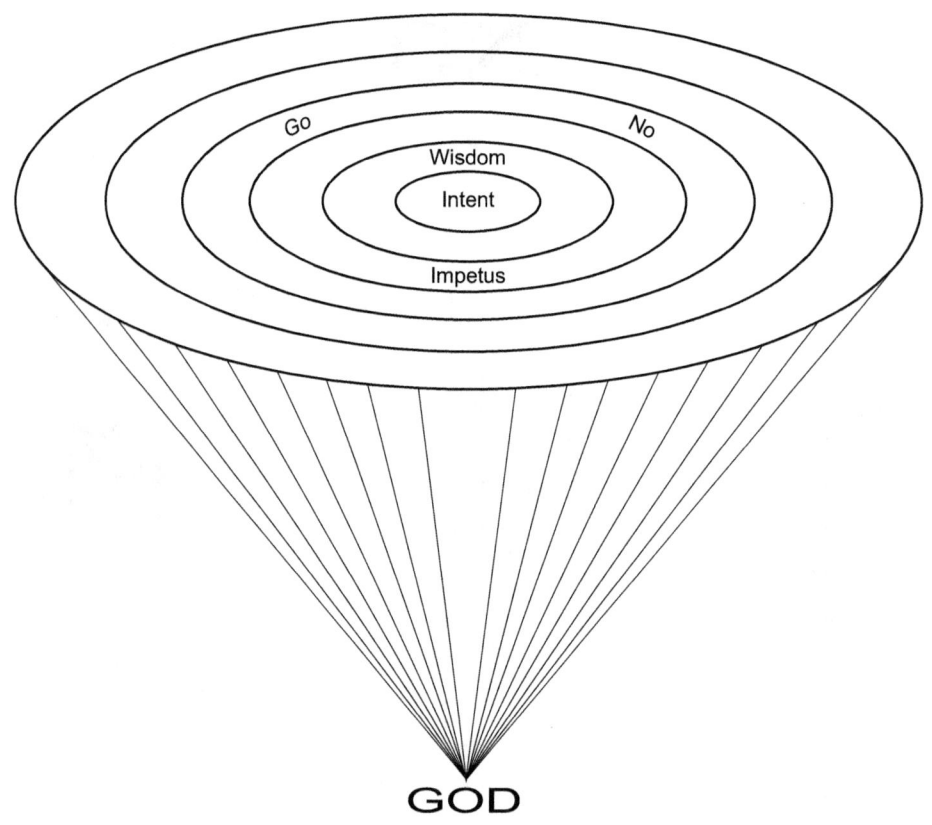

The seventh day is resting for the Lord your God, do not do any work… Do not murder. Do not get angry. Do not steal. Do not impoverish your fellow man with lying testimony. Do not covet your fellow man's home. Do not covet your fellow man's wife, his male servant, his female servant, his ox, his donkey, or anything else that your fellow man has.

Exodus 20:10-17,
Author's translation

Just say no.

Nancy Reagan

In the beginning, it was coffee. First, one cup at night, eventually seven. Like other achievement-oriented college students from the New York area, I did "whatever it took." When coffee didn't keep me awake, I moved to stronger chemicals. We didn't have Red Bull then, but if staying awake meant chewing coffee beans or ingesting over-the-counter or under-the-table stimulating drugs, I did it. Whatever it took.

Giving it our all and disregarding consequences is not unique to college students, of course. Despite "work-life balance" recently gaining traction, by many measures we still push ourselves beyond what is healthy for body, soul, and relationships. After all, we can *always* do better. The question is how much better we can do now and how quickly over what period of time and at what cost.

Wells Fargo is one of many examples of what happens when we measure the implementation of our intent with ever-increasing numbers, and we *Go* without God for the sake of the game and the gain. From 2002 to 2016, Wells Fargo increasingly operated in a culture of unregulated *Go*. To meet ever-larger sales quotas, personal bankers and loan officers had to sell more accounts and more financial products. As per the testimony of some former employees, there were so many products that they were sometimes required to sell more accounts than there were people in the towns that the branches "served."

Under *Go* policies, they brought in millions of dollars in fees. Great! However, to get there, thousands of employees contracted their customers for millions of financial products that the customers neither asked for nor needed. Creating fake social security numbers was not uncommon. To be clear, this is not just unethical, it is not just illegal; from the viewpoint of the customer, it is violent and abusive. They did the same thing I did as a college student, going from one cup of coffee to seven cups, to stronger chemicals. "Whatever it takes" took over and led to organizational illness.

At some point, No has to happen. In my case, all those ingested chemicals triggered arthritis and literally slowed my forward movement. For Wells Fargo, the US DOJ and SEC eventually fined them $3 billion. Consumers were brought to insolvency, employees lost their jobs, and Fargo lost consumer trust. Far-go went too far. Volkswagen, having programmed 11 million diesel vehicles to lie about their emissions, caused massive environmental pollution, was fined $15.3 billion, and lost public trust. If you don't choose to access No, life will force you into it.

Or so we colloquially speak. Truthfully, life does nothing to anyone. God is with us to allow our stronger values to win out. During the time of the Fargo and Volkswagen violations, our primarily No-oriented regulating bodies, propelled with moral impetus, acted upon the two companies to slow their *Go*. Hidden practices, once brought to light, thrust the organization deeper into No than it would have been had it entered No sufficiently from the start. In His working out of life on the grand scale that only He can, God supports our free will with free access to these modes. We access them either in humility or in selfishness. Humility demands a little pain upfront and delivers ongoing freedom; selfishness demands anxiety up front and delivers greater pain later.

> We access modes either in humility or in selfishness.

The need for No is a God-given protection in the form of a natural law; no one is exempt. Neither Wells Fargo nor VW nor I were in the real Go because we weren't working with God. Do you think VW's leadership had prayed about whether to authorize an emissions system that only functioned accurately when government inspectors were around? And the WF and VW incidents are just a couple of the significant number of unrestrained *Go* incidents that do not make such big splashes. "As this book goes to press, the US Consumer Financial Protection Bureau announced that it is suing Capital One bank for purposefully deceptive practices that cost depositors more than $2 billion. On a personal level, modal overreach stems from fear and selfish desire; at a corporate level it is also a result of lack of acculturating the value of humility. Without God's Wisdom, we go gaga in *Go* and do a nose dive that lands us in No.

No Defined

The mode of No is the spiritual space in which you naturally protect your organization from chaos, burnout, and self-destruction so that your Go functions can keep producing products and services.

No in organizations is God's subtle structure to promote thoughts, feelings, desires, surroundings, and purposes that contribute to order in ways that tend toward goodness and justice. Overall, No shows up as orderly resistance. In Go, God is full of life and joins us where we engage to do; in No, God helps us avoid chaos. Whereas Go contains a spirit of adventure, creation, and growth, No contains one of order and stability. While Go facilitates results (effectiveness), No eliminates drama and helps prevent mistakes (efficiency). Peace is actually a business benefit.

> **Action Step**
>
> Get quiet for a moment. Now ask God four questions:
>
> 1. Where in my own life and where in my organization does my push for *more* create disorder and toxic stress?
> 2. What improvements happen if I reduce stress?
> 3. Where, when, for how long, and in what ways should I regulate forward motion?
> 4. If I (and/or they) did less in that area, would I (and/or they) reduce or add to organizational value?

No in Your Organization

No is the focuser. It's in No that you protect organizational assets through diversification and by choosing *not* to acquire another company whose culture is too different from yours, no matter how good the numbers look now. In No, you prevent brand confusion by eliminating efforts that do not support core values. In No, you create a policy that limits the number of work hours, limits the objectives staff pursue, and turns managers into coaches to prevent employee burnout. To conserve assets, Purchasing sets guidelines. To prevent employees from getting too distracted, IT bars Facebook.

As with *Go*, No operates in functions, structure, culture, and people and has its valued place in the organizational lifecycle.

No functions. Here are examples of what are typically No functions:

- ***The Board.*** Some boards set strategic direction, but many just look to keep the organization from dissolving in disaster.

- **HR.** Keeping the organization from being sued and keeping employees playing well in the sandbox.
- *Accounting.* Avoid bad cash flow and IRS ire.
- *Finance.* Avoid insolvency. (If the culture is not fiscally conservative, Finance could be a *Go* function designed more specifically to generate wealth.)
- *Facilities.* Maintain workflow; avoid harm and lawsuits. A place for everything and everything in its place.
- *Security.* Avoid harm to persons, places, and information.
- *Legal counsel.* Protect the organization from anything that would lead to a lawsuit. Defend name and stock value.
- *Quality control.* Saying no to bad products.
- *Some management functions.* Moving people out of the wrong positions, reducing waste, and saying no to bad ideas.
- **PR.** Control damage from members saying or doing something seen as wrong. (Separate from PR's *Go* function of image creation.)
- **Purchasing.** Explain for the 1000th time why you can't sole source and generally say no to organizationally inefficient purchasing.
- *Compliance.* Avoid regulatory consequences.
- *Calendar.* Not a department, but everyone limits their actions on one thing to be able to do the next. If context is king, calendar is queen.

Just as there are No functions, there are also No-oriented structures, processes, personnel, and cultures.

No structures, No processes. A No-oriented structure exists where people have responsibilities without sufficient authority to fulfill them. This makes it more likely that they will reject new ideas, say "no" or "not now" rather than "yes" or "love it, let me get some buy-in." Advantage: keep the organization from going in too many directions. No-oriented processes prevent action until a list of criteria is met. It's automatically no until it's yes. Advantage: a No-process saves the organization when its people go too far since it provides the basis for firing them.

No people. Safety-oriented and alert for danger; No staff are oriented toward careful attention to detail and propriety. They tend to funnel actions through proven processes. They observe proper boundaries, whether in time, ethics, or finance. Advantage: No-mode people promote short-term efficiency.

No culture. The culture of No exists where the underlying assumption that guides emotional reactions and thoughtful policy is that it is better to be safe than sorry. It appears as a self-evident truth in No mode that pain is bad. The group self-identifies as the protector. The major concern is to save the organization from the reckless, the selfish, the lazy, the mean, and the misguided. A culture steeped in No might be highly appropriate, for instance, if your firm makes hazardous chemicals. People get irked by the DMV or City Hall or almost any monopoly in part because we think there should be a culture in *Go* but encounter a culture in No. Police, on the other hand, have a No culture that citizens get upset at when it moves too far into what seems to citizens to be *Go*. We want police to restrain others, and when it comes to us, they should restrain themselves. Cultures with a solid amount of No are often criticized by people with more progressive or *Go* sensibilities.

Cultures in No circle the wagons to protect themselves. On the front line, that often means that if it is 3:58 p.m., it is time to pack up one's stuff to protect one's personal time.

At the executive level, it can mean a tendency to overprotect the short-term bottom line and to obfuscate to protect the short-term image.

But No is hugely important, especially over time. Choices made in *Go* mode to meet a promised deadline or achieve a desired profit number can push past the No at their own peril and the peril of others. The executive decision to launch the space shuttle Challenger over the objection of its engineers, VW's decision to fake vehicles' emissions results, the understaffing and under-training at Union Carbide's Bhopal location, the exit door that flew off the Boeing aircraft, all of these were the result of No mode being too weak.

No and organizational lifecycle. In the previous chapter, we referred to four lifecycle phases.

1. Ideation & Formation
2. Production
3. Apex
4. Hardening of the Arteries

As place in the lifecycle changes, so does complexity. Managing complexity demands order. In each phase, the mode of No is accessed, but No strengthens and comes into its own in Apex. To reach Apex, No needs to brake *Go*. No will reduce production (effectiveness and short-term success) and increase regulation (efficiency and safety) to improve the likelihood of long-term success. No reduces short-term efficiency for individuals who tend to "do it my way," but it increases overall organizational efficiency.

To manage cash flow appropriately, you have to have income gained in *Go*, but you also have to have reigned-in expenses by operating in No. To expand consistently, you have to have a winning service (or product) and brand, which means having said no to a host of opportunities for which various people advocated. Breaking *Go* with No sets your organization up to sit solidly in the Apex lifecycle phase.

No Danger. No mode is meant to support growth by bounding it, in the same way river banks promote water-use by keeping water together. Over time, excess No extends the banks so far into the river that they dam it. The danger is not noticing when adding more No becomes an unbounded habit. At that point, No becomes an impediment to sustained growth. When No culture, structures, and processes become so strong that people are disincentivized from being curious, boundary-breaking, risk-taking, and innovative, those who operate in *Go* go elsewhere, and organizational hardening of the arteries sets in. Solution: keep strengthening your relationship with God so that He Who Loves You will be flowing in your veins (and in your mind) to awaken you to pivot and give you the conviction and strength to do it before hardening of the arteries sets in.

As you grow your relationship with God, if you wonder if a new pivot idea is from Him, re-examine the first three modes—Intent, Wisdom, and Impetus—to reassert their relevance to daily decision-making. Course correcting to keep the organization relevant and productive is a great challenge

> **No** *is necessary to enter the third phase the of organizational lifecycle, Apex.*

because the No mode has given you stability, security, and safety, all of which are hard to let go of. No has powerful advocates in the organization; there are people who state that the organization depends on No. But to survive, you have to stay dynamic, responsive, and innovative. Doing the right thing here means that the mode of No passes its zenith of importance. As with *Go*, the utility of No only continues in the long term if No is moderated. In beautiful poetic justice, you also say no to No.

No Customers

It is also key to consider your customers, clients, members, or patients as they enter No. At the time of this writing, Coca-Cola, Verizon, Unilever, Starbucks, and others have pulled their advertising from Facebook because of an unpopular stance that the Facebook organization took. Political pressure is accumulating against Amazon for its employee practices, just as it had for Wal-Mart years before. United Airlines is still receiving negative press long after its forcible removal of a doctor from an overbooked flight. These are all external stakeholders saying that they have triggers that send them into No in relationship to a business. If an organization's No is misaligned with the No sensibility of external stakeholders, it will suffer and need to adjust. A No organization can turn customers to No, which ultimately means... no customers.

Organizational Action Step

Consider whether your organization (unit, department, or team) relates well to No. Consider:

- location in the lifecycle,
- current strategic objectives, and
- short-term tactical needs.

Then look at:

- structures of authority and responsibility
- processes
- culture, including inter-unit communications,
- overall quantity of No,
- at whom No is directed,
- around what No is directed,
- when No becomes an imperative,
- who loses and benefits from having the organizational or team view be No.

No With God

With a big YES!, God created "*tohu-vavohu,*" a hurly-burly, formless structureless chaotic world. Then He said NO and made form, structure, separation, and order. Since then, we've spent a lot of time and effort rearranging the form of God's creation, building things up, and tearing things down. The transformative question of working with God is whether I say 'no' from a human point of view only or if I am willing to allow God to have a say in when I say 'no.' He invented the mode of No; within No, say yes to God, *then* act. Keep listening because you never know how He'll show up.

Two of the ways we see His action in No are ethics and holiness. Ethics and holiness help you be an organizational shepherd.

Ethics. When we look at the Bible, the foundation of Western ethics, we see that eight of the "Ten Commandments" operate in No[39]. As any parent knows, love can't operate without imposing order between people. When at least one person is <u>not</u> centered on deep peace, full self-awareness, love, and ethics, our group's effectiveness and personal safety are affected. Since there is often enough one person whose actions are shady, He sets healthy group boundaries. So should we.

Holiness. The divine expression of order is also tangibly experienced in holiness. This is more likely to happen for you than for your organization, but whoever you influence, influences your organization.

There is no chaos in holiness. Holiness brings you to reverent stillness and a proper relationship with God: we can't generate holiness; we can come nearer to *God's* holiness. We do that by intending to be with God and saying no to other things. God loves us so much that He's ready to share His perfection with us to the extent we can handle the experience of holiness.

To step into holiness, cultivate humility in front of God. Being humble because you believe it is morally superior to being egotistical does not necessarily lead to holiness. Holiness is felt in God's presence. Experiencing holiness, having a moral stance, and taking moral action are outcomes of God's truth in you. They are not outputs of self-effort. To get to holiness, cultivate humility in front of God. Look at God and recognize His greatness compared to your limited ability to command anything to happen. God is One; He speaks, and it is. Who are we in front of *That*? Be grateful,

---
[39]Seven are 'thou shalt not'; the positive commandment to keep the Sabbath is immediately explained by 'do not work.'

He loves you; be reverent, you can never compare. As it says in Psalms 46:10, "be still and know that I am God."

Humility in a relationship with God is a basic response to His presence; it's not a personality trait. Just ask Mark. Mark Whitacre's story provides a clear example of how God uses No personally, professionally, and organizationally in a unified whole.

Mark's Story, Continued

We left Mark in *Go* mode, achieving meteoric success. Painfully for Mark, his move from Intent to Impetus skipped Wisdom. Speedily *Go*-ing to achieve his intent, straightforward logic said to engage in international commodity price fixing. His two assumptions were that more is better, and you have to take it if you want it. Notice that a lack of wisdom leads to a lack of restraint. When his wife found out about the price fixing, she told him that if he did not tell the FBI, she would. Unlike Mark, she had a personal relationship with God that included humility, ethics, and holiness. Mark loved his wife, and she and God made sure that he would learn to live through Wisdom. Since he'd skipped that mode, he went directly to No. No would bring Mark wisdom.

At first, God gave him grace: the FBI offered to let him off the hook if he wore a wire and became an informant. While he agreed to those behaviors, his eyes missed the grace, and his heart and mind still skipped wisdom. While his left hand informed on his company's executives, his right hand embezzled $9,000,000. His self-justifying explanations for the extreme *Go* behavior did not change the fact that it was unmitigated *Go*. Two other executives were convicted, and now he was too. Unmoderated by Wisdom, his *Go* got him a year for every million dollars he took from others. God balanced Mark's *Go* with No. Lesson not learned, he spent his 40s in prison.

Going round and round in *Go,* always collecting $200 as it were, for Mark, the prospect of prison was an insurmountable shock. Between sentencing and prison, one night, alone in one of his many cars, despairing, he ricocheted into the negative extreme of No and tried to asphyxiate himself. But God was there, and Mark survived. Before Mark entered prison, God sent him a scientist, and together they examined the possibility of God's existence. In prison, a former White House Counsel under President Nixon, one who had also snapped from excess *Go* down into prison No, visited Mark. He brought books and articles, and over the course of time, they talked about God and life. Mark realized a humble stance and gave his life to Jesus. Everything changed. Over time, Mark accessed Wisdom.

Accepting a long moment in No, Mark was now able to stop. What he found when he stopped was that he and his intent were no longer the measure of all things; God exists. God lives. God loves. Mark found holiness. *Go* now needed to have a purpose bigger than Mark; he wanted it to have God's purpose. Now, with wisdom, humility, and a sense of the holy, Mark returned to *Go.* He helped fellow prisoners get their GED. Instead of leading from above, he led from beside. His inmate teammates respected him, and the FBI fought for his early release. Once you give God the choice of which mode is for you at any given time, the mode no longer owns you; you are free to move on.

As we'll see when we finish Mark's story in Part Two, his surrender to God's will in No had astounding consequences not only personally, but also professionally. But for now, the important part is that Dr. Whitacre, bereft of everything and stuck in prison, was now filled with a huge sense of God's love, a huge YES that only could have come to him when he accepted, honored, and entered God's No.

Mark's experience can help us understand Jesus' famous speech that gave a great new vista to those stuck in No (Matthew 5):

> Blessed are the poor in spirit, for theirs is the kingdom of heaven. Blessed are those who mourn, for they shall be comforted. Blessed are the meek, for they shall inherit the earth. Blessed are those who hunger and thirst for righteousness, for they shall be satisfied.
> —Matthew 5:3-6 (ESV)

Blessed are those held in No, for their freedom comes from God.

Chapter Six

PRIME

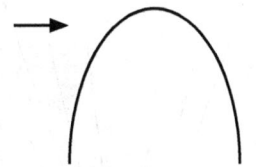

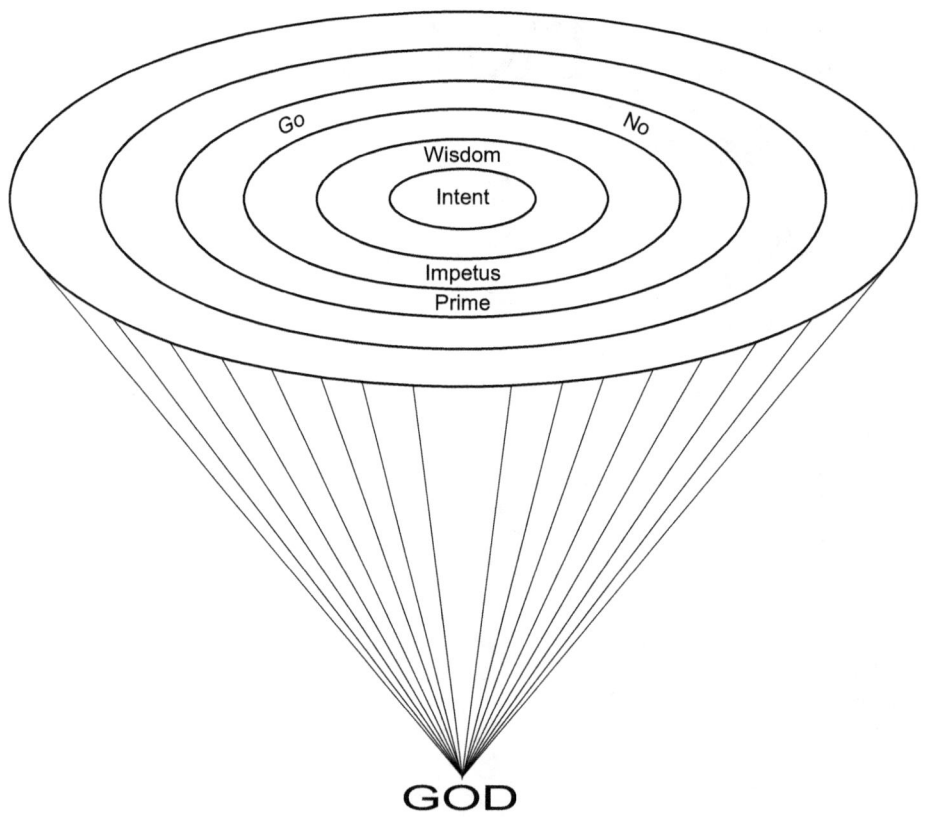

*"Humility must always be the portion
of any man who receives acclaim
earned in blood of his followers
and sacrifices of his friends."*

General Dwight David Eisenhower,
having completed his role as
Supreme Allied Commander in Europe.
London, June 12, 1945

While in the mode of No, you formed order from chaos. You increased efficiencies and reduced burnout. Excellent. Now what? More No?

No. To maintain momentum, you say no to No. If you keep increasing No, you look at any change through the lens of the past and say, "That's not how we do it." Consistency becomes king, process becomes prince, and efficiency is all. Instead of getting a standing ovation for innovation, you get a boring No-vation. Bureaucracy blooms, rules rule, talent quits. Wave market relevance goodbye.

But how do you say no to No without unleashing *Go* chaos? You expand your perspective, one that allows you to decide when being in *Go* or No is appropriate. For that, God gave us the mode of Prime.

What Prime Isn't. This sixth mode is not a prime number, nor is it the Fed's interest rate. "Prime" does not mean primary, as in first. It also does not mean strongest, as in 'he's in his prime.' Neither does Prime here refer to a lifecycle phase.

What Prime Is. Prime is where you stand beyond *Go* and No, recognize the value of each, and decide which is the appropriate mode for whom, when, how long, how much, and for what purpose. In making that decision, you include your intent and wisdom. In Prime, God helps us be, see, and act cogently amidst complexity. In Prime, you coordinate disparate actions that integrate your organization's internal and external environments to fulfill your intent. You balance and sometimes even integrate competing stakeholder needs. Daily, you increase, reduce, or maintain the importance of one or another of the previous five modes to generate long-term success. One of Prime's keywords is integration.

Prime's other two keywords are awareness and agility. *Awareness* is straightforward: stay awake, see what is going on or isn't, and delegate urgent tasks to deal with the important. Awareness is a state of honesty that demands humility.

Agility is balancing competing values over time. Though balance happens over time, at any particular time, you move out towards an extreme rather than in toward moderation. You might, for instance, decide to maintain an unusually high or low-risk position. As long as you make sure that the decision passes through Intent for Purpose and Wisdom for a reality check and that you'll have enough impetus to change it in *Go* and *No*, you are in Prime.

Prime example: Let's take a plane flight for example. A trained and experienced pilot utilizes Prime to follow the flight plan and stay responsive to conditions. She monitors weather, staff, passengers, mechanics, geolocation, surrounding aircraft, etc., and makes in-the-moment operational decisions.

> *Prime's 3 Keys:*
> - *Awareness*
> - *Agility*
> - *Integration*

As she pilots our long-distance flight, a passenger becomes highly agitated and the doctor two rows back diagnoses peritonitis (severe appendicitis). He says that if the passenger is not operated on within an hour, the passenger will probably die. In Prime, the pilot speeds the situation through the five modes.

1. **Intent:** Keep passengers alive.
2. **Wisdom:** Keeping one passenger alive justifies a change in everyone's flight plan.

3. **Impetus:** Save human life *now*.
4. **No:** End the current flight plan.
5. *Go*: Turn the plane toward a hospital.

Note that *Go* and No switched the access order according to situational logic. Staying awake and agile means you can use linear process thinking but, don't let it use you.

With the authority of Prime, she integrates the five modes by communicating. She tells the co-pilot to find the nearest hospital and communicates the reroute to the airport nearest to that hospital. She announces to the passengers that due to a sudden acute illness onboard (context—**Wisdom**), it is regrettable but urgent (passion—**Impetus**) that the plane be diverted to a new destination (**Intent**). She reduces thrust (**No**) on the port side and increases it in the starboard engines (*Go*). A few passengers grumble, but there is no lawsuit because, in **Prime**, she communicates the wisdom of the change. She does what leaders do: she successfully moves the plane from one reality (plane flying from Point A to Point B) to a new reality (plane flying from Point A to Point Q). Passenger survives and helps the airline by providing a glowing testimonial that PR spins into its new branding effort. In Prime, agility ability is strength.

Now, a question. Do you think that God can help your ability to obtain and process information? Do you think that God would help you? If you don't want His help, He probably won't help. Too bad for the passenger. His human creations have free will. But if you build a relationship through prayer and responding to promptings, even if you jump into focused pilot mode and don't think to pray anything other than "God help," you will most likely respond to His promptings and be greeted by surprisingly helpful circumstances. By this point in your having practiced talking with God, you wouldn't ascribe perfect circumstances to fate or chance or the universe or luck or good karma. By now, you can see the working hand of God. Stars aren't lucky, they are stars; thank God.

Prime Leadership

Prime mode facilitates an expansive view of options and your ability to exercise freedom of choice. In that sense, it is a global, neutral, utilitarian mode. However, in the global mode of Prime, excellent executives will still tend toward whichever mode is most natural to them, their 'go-to' mode. Some will consider things for longer; some will execute more quickly. Executives rely on their strengths, but Prime demands that they also stay aware of their blind spots and balance them by developing teams whose members have abilities that the executives do not.

As a Prime executive or entrepreneur, you might:

- take time for strategic planning (**Intent**),
- conduct pre-mortems (**Wisdom**),
- give inspiring talks (**Impetus**),
- publicly congratulate the VP of Strategic Development on the success of their new initiative (***Go***),
- fight off a hostile takeover (**No**),
- or negotiate a deal with the union (**Prime**).

Prime leadership is complex and challenging. Others deep in any of the previous modes have the privilege of seeing the world primarily through the lens of that mode. They do their job by evaluating information through that one lens. For instance, a SCRUM evangelist in Impetus, tries to get everyone together in forward motion. Even if their direction is not the most useful or aligned with organizational intent, it still *feels* right because 'the team is working together at a fast pace.' In Prime, you wrestle with competing values. People primarily in one of the other five modes may devalue your decision for not being better at how it is they see things. Good communication can minimize but not eliminate this. Tough luck on them; you're in your Prime.

> *A moment of Prime saves time.*

Leadership Action Step

A moment of Prime saves time. Take time to analyze your organization mode by mode. Here are some starter questions.

- **Intent.** How well does the project's "why" support the strategic plan?
- **Wisdom.** Is efficiency or effectiveness more important here?
- **Impetus.** Too much fire or too little?
- *Go.* What should be moving faster?
- **No.** What danger signals am I hearing?

Of course, before you ask yourself those questions, ask God for help with seeing clearly. After you have thought about your business mode by mode, try using the prayer list in Appendix B, which walks you through the modes prayer by prayer. God is for you. Once you put Him ahead of you, He will also be active in your organization. Maybe He already is.

Prime in the Organizational Lifecycle

Accessing Prime happens in each of the lifecycle phases, but the organization most frequently accesses the mode of Prime in the Apex stage. In Apex, the scope of considerations demands that the leader spend more time in Prime.

Larger Apex Organizations: 3-mode Prime. The larger the organization, the more complex, and the more you will lead through the three abstract modes: Intent, Wisdom, and Impetus. You may, for instance, operate in these first three modes to emphasize lobbying activities. Lobbying garners support for your organization's intent (**Intent**). It gets legislators to support the organization's values and methods (**Wisdom**). It also creates legislative initiatives that open a beneficial path for your organization (**Impetus**).

Smaller Apex Organizations: 2-mode Prime. The smaller the organization, the fewer the operations units, product lines, and so on, and the greater the need for executives to be in the two concrete modes, *Go* and No. Rather than lobbying, you will more likely change internal policy (**Go**) to match new regulations (**No**) and keep going.

Whatever the size, or place in the lifecycle, in Prime, leadership decides which ones of the five modes get how much of which resources and when.

Prime Organizational Functions

Along with its place in leadership and lifecycle, Prime operates within departments and functions and also manages conflict between them. First, let's look at Prime functions, then Prime in conflict management, and then we'll see God in Prime.

C-Suite. Maintains maximal organizational *Go* with the minimum necessary No. Translates the organization's intent into strategic objectives and organizational accomplishments with decision-making, storytelling, and resource allocation. Weighs short-term tactical pressures against long-term strategic objectives.

IT. Provides information across silos, allowing *Go* and No functions to interact with each other and with organizational wisdom to help translate intent into concrete implementation.

Internal Communications. Reminds silos of organizational intent, helping explain to each silo why the others also deserve to have their way.

Some manager functions. Balancing the voices of various team members. Manages bi-directional vertical information flow within silo to increase the effectiveness of decision-making and/or implementation. Balances *Go-No* in the short term.

Operations. Depending on the culture, operations teams might lean towards 'get it done' and be more in the mode of *Go*, or 'keep operations as efficient as possible' and be more in the mode of *No*. But most are awake to achieving both values.

Systems Improvement. In larger organizations, there are likely one or more teams devoted to continuous systems improvement. A change anywhere inside or outside the organization may bring complications that slow down delivery of value, and these systems improvers speed it up again.

Prime and Go-No Conflict

Sitting in Prime helps you limit *Go-No* conflict to the minimum level necessary for sustained growth. Too little conflict means the organization is not confronting important issues that will surface and be more challenging to deal with if ongoingly disregarded. Too much conflict and wasting energy on infighting lowers morale, efficiency, and effectiveness. Thinking, praying, going for a swim, or talking to someone who stands in Prime will show you how to decrease conflict.

Managing *Go-No* Conflict Through Culture. Managing *Go-No* conflict is made easier through a culture of honesty and mutual respect. Honesty is not just a soft skill used in good communication; it is realistic data analysis based on sufficient information. For instance, staff often cut corners with data entry because it doesn't pass the "what's in it for me" WIFM test. This puts staff and management in quiet conflict, while insufficient information from the point of purchase reduces organizational effectiveness and creates a defect in the organization's structural integrity. Integrating staff's needs into the software redesign restores information flow, structural integrity, and organizational effectiveness. In Prime, you integrate the bigger picture—in this case, staff's needs—into the operational level by developing a culture of respect that allows honesty. That way, when you send a survey, they believe you when you say it's anonymous; when you say, "We made the best decision possible under the circumstances," they are more likely to believe you.

Prime humility for founders. If you are a small business entrepreneur, it feels like everything is on your shoulders. Your intent, wisdom, impetus, and *go* drove your company to success. Great! For you, however, the founder's trap is waiting. To avoid getting stuck in this trap, you must have a particular aspect of Prime honesty: humility.

Getting stuck in the founder's trap happens when you don't revisit your original intent. You know what to do and how to do it. But sooner or later, "how to do things" is based on a relationship to an environment that already changed, while you are slower than your younger employees in seeing that the change is as profound as it really is. Conflict results with those you hire because they know the environment differently and have new tools to address it. To navigate the founder's trap, honestly and openly re-examine your intent and wisdom. If you don't, your teammates or competitors will do it for you. Listen to them without pride. To operate in Prime, you need careful ears and great honesty. All of that totals up to one thing: humility.

Prime God

To interact with God around whatever you and/or your organization are going through, try any or all of the following.

1. **Talk to Him, tell Him how you see the situation**
   - <u>Acknowledge</u> your need.
   - <u>Request</u> that He help you sort things out.
   - <u>Tell</u> Him exactly what you see. When doing so, don't blame anyone; take responsibility.
   - <u>Listen</u> for response or resonance inside yourself and out there in your world. Take a walk alone, without a phone. Trust that the answer will show up in time, even if it's 'just in time.'
2. **Seek His wisdom**
   - <u>Pray</u>: Acknowledge to Him that He is great and you are not much by comparison. Thank Him for previous and current goodness. Ask Him, mode by mode, to show you what you are missing there. Then, go about your business; notice when you or

someone with you had good insight, and thank God for that.
- Speak with God-solid people.
- Read the Bible slowly and talk about it with those you trust and respect. Use an AI app or a search engine to find places in the Bible that relate to the essence or key aspects of the situation. E.g., "trickery in the Bible" or "offense in the Bible" or "scarcity in the Bible," etc.

3. **Seek His grace**
   - Pray: Get humble, make your request, and let Him know that you'll be grateful regardless of how grace shows up or doesn't.
   - Thank Him (for what He does for you and others) ongoingly, even if it is painful.
   - Praise Him (for being who He is) ongoingly. Praise is like thanks but on steroids since it involves the love of Him and His wondrousness, His greatness, His goodness, (and on and on) rather than just gratitude for what He does for you.
   - Open your heart and eyes to loving others.
   - Ask for His help to grace others, then go be a blessing to others without taking credit.
4. **Risk following His lead,** even if this might initially feel awkward.
5. **Establish, stabilize, and expand** your two-way communication with God by building relationships with others who are doing the same. Dare even to find a church where you can sense God in the people who go there.

Most likely, His voice will sound exactly like your own, but He will say things you weren't thinking of. He can also use your pain to grab your attention (remember Mark

Whitacre?). Or you may be reading, and some words impact you with unusual immediacy and depth. God often whispers, it's a clear and loud statement for those with ears to hear.

Discern and learn. In all these things, it is up to you to discern if it is the voice of God. Maybe it is your personal *'this is what I want, and I'm just going to believe it is God speaking so I can do what I want'* voice. Maybe it is any of the many other voices that are neither yours nor God's. If you are to benefit from God's counsel, it has to be *God's* counsel. Although there is no guarantee that you discern well, especially at the start, the effort is incredibly worth it.

How does one discern? There is no quick fix or silver bullet. As with any skill, discernment gets built through attention, repetition, honesty, humility, courage, obedience to what you believe is God's voice, sizing up both short and long-term results, and frequent engagement. If you try to discern God's voice while holding selfish motivation and pretending to yourself that you aren't selfish, you won't succeed; God knows what you really want, and He responds to honesty. Amid pressures, it gets tricky. But with commitment and grace, it can be done. It's wise to ask Him for grace.

For encouragement, here is an example of someone who discerned well.

Gideon's Story[31]

Gideon was the youngest son of the head of the Ephraim tribe in ancient Israel. A mid-sized group with about 40,000

---

[31] From chapters 6-8 in the Book of Judges. Apart from being an awesome page-turner, the story is packed with key lessons for executives working with God.

people, for illustrative purposes, we'll call it Ephraim Corp. Gideon's dad was Chairman of the Board and CEO, and Gideon was a junior VP. Midianites and Amalekites—the Amazons and Walmarts of the day—were eating Israel's market share. They were not just metaphorically 'making a killing', but actually killing Israelites; they meant business.

Though a part of Holy Israel, Inc., Ephraim Corp's SOP was standard: sacrifice to the Canaanite deity Baal to get bottom-line results. They saw Baal as their rainmaker and gave him huge bonuses to increase their numbers. Gideon's CEO dad thought God was just a silent partner, whereas the local deity was the managing partner. The CEO had a fundamental lack of clear vision. God messaged Gideon: tear down Dad's altar to Baal and replace it with an altar to Himself. In business speak, God told Gideon to change the company culture.

Gideon wasn't so sure. That kind of task, for one person? What VP wouldn't calculate the consequences of failure? God's messenger found Gideon hiding amidst farming equipment, playing individual contributor, and evading the Midianites. Gideon was literally separating the wheat from the chaff, a perfect metaphor for the decision he now faced. Was he going to be wheat and sustain his people, or chaff to be blown aside by the Midianite winds?

Decision time and the power of discernment: even though Gideon saw himself as weak, *he knew God was real* and discerned the difference between his strength and God's. He traded false humility (fear) for real humility (love) and let God's strength in. He removed the altar to Baal and replaced it with an altar to God. Baal worship took a hit, and Baal's stock price dropped to pennies on the dollar. Gideon took Ephraim Corp private and made God the majority owner.

Unsurprisingly, the stockholders (townsfolk) were ready to kill him. Literally. But since he responded to God's voice, God was with him. Gideon communicated a new set of core values and reframed Ephraim Corp's culture. Instead of being fired (stoned to death), he dressed himself in God's authority and became Gideon, CEO.

God gave Gideon a strategic plan. Discerning that it was God talking, he called several tribes together, creating a cartel that beat the Midianites' hostile takeover attempt. They captured enemy territory (munched Midianite market share) and much booty (profits and stock price jumped). In Prime, Gideon navigated a gauntlet of decisions about resource allotment, risk assumption, supply chain management, whom to trust, and other tactical issues. Sometimes, he consulted with God; sometimes, he just went ahead, and God backed him up. Gideon became CEO for life as Ephraim Corp, and the parent holding company, Holy Israel, Inc., enjoyed success during his forty-year tenure.

How's that for *more*? Gideon could work with God at that level of risk because he accepted responsibility for a ridiculously challenging situation. He could do that because he knew God was with him. He knew the voice of God. He was clear on what God's voice was, what his voice was, and what voices were other people's. Listening to God—as unpopular then as it is now—catapulted Gideon to a new spiritual station and a qualitatively richer career. The result was a military, monetary, ethical, and spiritual renewal for all of Ephraim and the Israelite people (insert *name of your business* here).

This kind of thing can happen when one is awake enough to discern and humble enough to implement God's counsel. With God, anything is possible. Robust and humble leadership and God converge in Prime for greater organizational success in navigating complexity. God always loves. So, keep going, get humble, and ask Him for help with complex situations. Ask Him to guide your intent, grant you wisdom, and give you impetus. Seek His counsel on when and where to change *Go* or *No*. Operate with Him in Prime and rejoice, knowing that your life is bigger for including God in it, day by day, decision by decision, action by action. Pray, listen, discern, and act in your organization. The challenge brings surprising results and greater personal richness.

It Sounds Like That's It. Is It?

And if you do all that, grow and succeed on multiple levels, and still want more? There is always more. It's on the other side of a door that sits just after the next fork in the road. When you want still more, turn the page.

Chapter Seven

THE DOOR

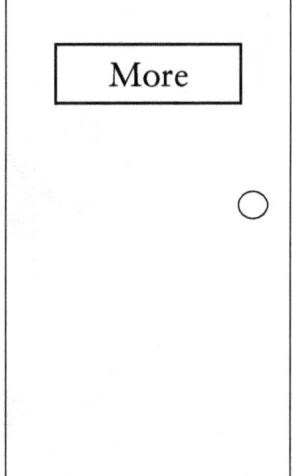

Ask,
And it will be given to you.

Seek,
And you will find.

Knock,
and it will be opened to you.

For everyone who asks receives,
and the one who seeks finds,
and to the one who knocks,
it will be opened.

Matthew 7:7-8
(ESV)

You walk down a busy street. You've done it a hundred times. This time, though, a hulk of a man saunters toward you and stops about a foot directly in front of you. You stop and look up. He stares straight into your eyes, pulls a gun from his waistband, and sticks it in your gut. You feel like you were pushed out of a plane without a parachute. "This is a stickup, Mister (or Ma'am)," he says, "your goal or your soul."

Of course, you give the man your goal. He takes it, turns, and leaves you goalless. "Phew, I got away with my soul," you think. Eventually, you calm down. Then another thought jumps into your mind and stops right there: "No goal. What now?"

Before you adopt another goal, stop for a moment with me. Survey what you have. You have the chair you're sitting in, the bed you lay on, a refrigerator with food and drink, probably a family, money in the bank, and at least one table in your home. You have language. Your body functions (more or less). And you have a relationship with God.

Maybe you remember that you want greater success. That's fine. But <u>at this very moment</u>, you are successful; you are complete. If you stop now, for a moment, and release whatever image you have of your future, if you know that God is with you unless you are showing Him the back of your neck instead of your face, you will feel the naked, peaceful state of existence: completeness and joy. Or maybe you step even closer to God, close enough to experience His majesty. As soon as you touch that moment of connection with God, you feel that you need nothing because you are already the recipient of unbelievable goodness to which you have no claim. Regardless of what happens around you, even to your legacy, your soul now demands that you live in the truth that your accomplishments are nothing compared to living in the presence of God.

Next steps. You walk on along the road as the busy street vaguely hums, out of focus, around you. Life's integration with the truth of completion and wholeness begins.

Of course, we know that while we are complete, we can also *feel* incomplete by underperforming on measures of success that we assign to ourselves. Many people adopt measures that compare themselves to others, and with nearly eight billion people to compare to, that's a superb recipe for discontentment and anxiety.

Good news #1: when you are with God in the moment, you are in the presence of pure goodness. This choice during a phase of discontentment is available: either stick to my criteria of success and recreate that set of circumstances in which I was happy, or let the criteria go, strengthen my relationship with God, and let Him grow me into the unknown *more*. Good news #2: you adopted the measures; you can drop them. To drop them, though, you need to face yourself.

One of my favorite lines in the entire New Testament is the first thing the Gospel of John records Jesus as saying. Jesus is strolling around beyond the Jordan River, that physical and metaphoric dividing line between the land of the people of God and all other lands. He passes within eyesight of John the Baptist. The baptizer exclaims to two of his disciples something like: 'Look, there goes the messiah!' Rich with excitement, the disciples catch up to Jesus so they can ask where he is staying. But before they can ask, Jesus turns around, faces them, and asks: "What do you seek?"[32] BAM. The Bible doesn't record lots of small talk for Jesus. God is not rushed, but He is supremely concise. He just asked them what the goal of their lives is.

---

[32] John 1:38 MEV

> **Action Step**
>
> Ask yourself, what *do* I seek?
> Answer the question.
> Then, ask yourself if your answer involves you controlling your circumstances.
> If it does, ask yourself if you want God and His glory to be your experience, your "land."
> Many religious and even spiritual people seek both. But we can't hold on to both. Maintain control, and God's glory will walk on by. Hold on to God, and you surrender your control over circumstances. You can't have both.
> This is the same question as "Your goal or your soul?" What *do* you seek? It's your stickup moment.

The Fork

What's down road #1? If you choose to continue as before, you'll continue to cycle through the six modes. You'll find a new intent and seek wisdom around that new intent. Being innocently hopeful, you'll find new impetus and tell everyone, "I'm ____ (*fill in the blank' with a gerund, such as starting, creating, having, building, making, investing, doing, etc*)." Then, you engage Go, No, and Prime.

When you talk to God, you ask for what you want for yourself, your family, your friends, your organization. God wants good for you and yours, so there's nothing wrong with that. It's good. Still, this is a bit like asking God for help rearranging your furniture while ignoring His offer of a better home.

What's down road #2? A whole new estate on God's perfect property is yours. *If you want it.* As Jesus said, "everyone who asks receives, and the one who seeks finds, and to the one who knocks, it will be opened." (Matthew 4:7-8)

It's fine to start walking the second road tentatively to see if it's right for you. But at some point, you must confront the question: Do you want to peek at God from behind a bush that is *not* burning with God's good fire, or are you ready to walk into God's house and stay? Are you content with your life and leadership being improved, or do you want them elevated to a new plane of operation? That is the only question at the fork in the road.

As you consider the question, see if you might relate to another Ask-Seek-Knock traveler. Meet Kurt.

> *Do you want your life and leadership elevated to a new plane of operation?*

Kurt's Story

Working hard *and* smart, Kurt Riegelman rose through the ranks with speed. He started as a contract manager for Hughes Space & Communications. Metaphorically and literally, not even the sky was the limit. After a decade in aerospace, he co-founded an inventory control corporation. Bringing in high-flying customers such as Boeing, Northrop-Grumman, and United Airlines, Kurt lived a lot in *Go*. As Director and Chairman of the Board, he also guided his company in Prime. Simultaneously, Kurt took a position as VP of American Sales at the world's leading satellite company, Intelsat. He soon became SVP of Global Sales for Intelsat. Then SVP, Sales *and* Marketing. Just fifty and the world his oyster.

His success wasn't only due to his smarts, hard work, social skills, and physical stature. When he was young, he adopted a deep intent: "Never quit." He applied the intent with Marine-like discipline. However hard it got, men of lesser grit might give up, but he would not. Give it to Kurt, and it will get done.

Kurt married a wonderful woman, fathered two promising children, went to church, and gave to charity. He prayed regularly, read the Bible, and did his best to live in such a way he hoped would give Jesus a reason to smile and say to him: "'Well done, good and faithful servant! You have been faithful with a few things; I will put you in charge of many things. Come and share your master's happiness!'"[33]

The fork. For the five years before Kurt added the marketing portfolio to his SVP Sales job, Intelsat's sales curve was headed up and to the right. It was the undisputed leader in the satellite space. Six months later, not so much. Several new trends now made their impact felt:

1. Production improvements in the satellite industry created overwhelming supply.
2. Developing countries now had access to undersea cable and overland fiber optics that reduced satellite demand.
3. Many countries that had been satellite consumers had turned to building their own and selling excess below market rates.

Things changed. Intelsat's sales curve flattened, and revenue dropped. Kurt was responsible for revenue, so when

---
[33] John 1:38 MEV

people with budgets asked themselves where to get a satellite, he saw it as his job to make sure the answer was: "Intelsat." But that was okay; it wasn't Kurt's first challenge.

He tried various approaches to increasing sales and revenue. After six months, there was no change. It weighed on him, which weighed on his marriage and family. He felt the fate of the company on his shoulders. But true to his principal principle, he did not quit. After another six months, the curve worsened. By now, he felt the pressure.

Of course, there was an obvious answer to all the stress of course, obvious to his wife at least: let it go. But Kurt's identity was wrapped up in the discipline of not being a quitter. Letting go was quitting; quitting was a moral failure. He soldiered on, casting about as best as that very talented man could, seeking a solution. Valiantly, he tried to get sales moving.

The choice. Two years of the pressure of juggling sales, marketing, family, and church. Pressure caused friction and increased heat. You can imagine his thoughts. How can I let all these good people down? What if I can't do this? People wouldn't be able to count on me. Career and worth? Kurt was looking at losing everything he had put so much effort into building.

His space sufficiently contracted, he had to decide. Stay on top of this, find a solution in *Go* while risking more stress to his family, or let it go and enter a risky future. With enough pressure, people either break apart or, like carbon, become a diamond. He was in it together with his wife, and God was there, but still, it was his to choose and his to lose. He emptied his heart to God and received perspective on his intent as a gift in return. He received wisdom. Kurt let go of the job.

He stopped trying to be the person he believed he should be. He gave up his narrow focus on career success. He sought and submitted himself to God's perspective. He told Jesus he would do *whatever* He wanted, even if that meant a lifestyle trim. He had knocked on the door and received God's response. He told the CEO that he had done his best and should pass the portfolio on to someone more qualified. With a now deeper trust in God, Kurt chose obedience to the Truth, to God, and he quit being obedient to never quitting. He was free.

We'll pick up Kurt's story again in the next chapter. For now, let's suffice with the picture of rejoicing in heaven. I can't imagine, but the words "Well done, good and faithful servant" were ever applied so wholeheartedly to Kurt's life as in that moment of humble obedience in giving up his own intent and letting God's intent will out. The content of Kurt's business was now essentially none of Kurt's business. Kurt Riegelman made a regal man's choice.

Let's re-examine the quote about the prophet Elisha that we read in *Go*. There is more to it than first meets the eye.

> "When Elisha entered the house, behold the boy was dead, laid out on his bed. So he entered and shut the door behind them and prayed to the Lord. Then… the flesh of the child became warm… then the boy opened his eyes."[34]

Like Elisha, Kurt had to close the door behind him to allow God to bring new life out of old.

THE DOOR

Let's say that, like Kurt, you choose to do God's will rather than have God help you do your will. At the fork,

---
[34] 2 Kings 4: 32-35 (NASB)

you choose that other road and start walking. There, on the road, you see a door. Do you knock?

The air on the other side of the door is air touched by God. In that world, you still do what you do as a CEO, executive, or entrepreneur. It's just that here, your life is fundamentally no longer yours. What is here belongs to God. You are part of God's business—and what a privilege!—but the 'you' would not be the 'you' that you were before. Kudos go to God, not to you. Shedding the weight of self-government, you would be simpler and lighter. Beyond that door, God governs; you 'do the do' for Him and with Him. The privilege of living life moment to moment with Him, free and humble, is yours. His ever-present, never-selfish love is yours. Peace is yours. Prizes and surprises, too, some of which will taste sweet, some sour. But they are from Him and build a life of increasing strength. Along with it all, joy and a deep peace, even at work.

God invites you to let the burden of control be His. Words from God, through a psalmist who opened the door: *"I removed his shoulder from the burden... You called in trouble, and I delivered you. Open your mouth wide, and I will fill it... I will satisfy you with honey out of the rock."*[35]

It's your time. Will you give it to God? God relishes the wholehearted, so be real. It is either time for you to give your time to God, or it isn't. But, as Rabbi Hillel famously said: "If not now, when?"[36]

JESUS: FRIEND OR LORD?

We still have one last thing to clarify: Who is God? God is impossible to define, that's true. But you will likely lean

---
[35] Psalm 81: 6-10 (WMB)
[36] Talmud, Pirkei Avot 1:15

toward one of two different stances: Friend or Lord. If you are asking Jesus to set you up for a relationship with I-Will-Be so that you can survive and thrive, know in front of Whom you stand. Or kneel. Or lie face down on the ground. Or be embraced by. Or dance with. Is Jesus your friend, or is He your Lord?

Friend. God is your sweetest friend. He creates opportunities for you and blesses you with the desires of your heart in things big and small. King David saw that relationship this way:

> Trust in the Lord and do good; dwell in the land and cultivate faithfulness. Delight yourself in the Lord and He will give you the desires of your heart. Commit your way to the Lord, trust also in Him, and He will do it… Rest in the Lord and wait patiently for Him; do not fret because of him who prospers in his way. Because of the man who carries out wicked schemes. Cease from anger and forsake wrath; do not fret; it leads only to evildoing. For evildoers will be cut off, but those who wait for the Lord, they will inherit the land. Yet a little while and the wicked man will be no more, and you will look carefully for his place and he will not be there. But the humble will inherit the land and will delight themselves in abundant prosperity.[37]

There is no friend better than God. No friend more steadfast, none kinder, none more capable. This relationship is sweet and tender, like the one that King Solomon described

---
[37]Psalms 37: 3-11 NASB

in the Song of Solomon, and it is replete with intimate dating that leads to marriage. It was God-my-Friend who told my wife to get the herring. A relationship with God-the-Friend tastes sweet. With Friends, we can face anything.

Lord. Then, sometimes, we face the other face of God. God also tastes bitter. God also does not at all feel like your friend and can, on the face of things, feel like your enemy. It's tough love; really tough. How much are you ready to lose? He who is beyond death is not moved by what you think is a big deal. This is not a relationship of equals. God is terrible. Not in a moral way, but literally: He inspires terror. God is so far beyond your identity that carrying your identity to face God is a terribly bad idea; not wise. Remember Proverbs 9:10, "Fear of the Lord is the beginning of wisdom."

Here is the prophet Isaiah's experience of meeting God: "Woe to me!" I cried. "I am ruined! For I am a man of unclean lips, and I live among a people of unclean lips, and my eyes have seen the King, the Lord Almighty."[38]

Not only is God terrible, but He sometimes requires us to endure pain for the good of others. God tells Ezekiel:

> "Now lie on your left side and place the sins of Israel on yourself. You are to bear their sins for the number of days you lie there on your side. I am requiring you to bear Israel's sins for 390 days—one day for each year of their sin. After that, turn over and lie on your right side for 40 days—one day for each year of Judah's sin… I will tie you up with ropes so you

---

[38]Isaiah 6: 1-6 NIV

won't be able to turn from side to side until the days of your siege have been completed.[39]

God loved His people by reproaching them, and Ezekiel had to endure God's love. "Love" here is clearly not what we mean when we say, "I love my Yeti mug." It's absolutely not a feel-good love. You are not Ezekiel, but at some point, you will have to face this face of God and suffer. But having given up your rights at the door, you will suffer *for* Him, and He will be there with you. And it will be okay. It will be more than okay; it will be very good. How else does a leader move their business through internal and external challenges if they haven't had to endure pain and stay the course while remaining steadfast and clear?

Don't try to pour yourself a nice hot toddy and tell a story about a wrathful Old Testament God who a loving New Testament God replaced. Remember the Jesus who throws down the money-changers' tables and whips them with a cat-o'-nine tails? Or the Jesus who withers the fruitless fig tree? Who called the leading religious figures of his day "whitewashed tombs" and "hypocrites" to their faces? Or the Jesus who said he came not for peace but as a sword?

John the Apostle recorded this about 'judgment day':

> Then the kings of the earth, the rulers, the generals, the rich people, the powerful people, the slaves, and the free people hid themselves in caves and in the rocks on the mountains. They called to the mountains and the rocks, "Fall on us. Hide us from the face of the One who sits on the throne and from the anger

---
[39]Ezekiel 4: 4-7 NLT

of the Lamb! The great day for their anger has come, and who can stand against it?"⁴⁰

Clearly, this is not a picture-book fluffy lamb. He is not the "my friend" God you can't wait to hang out with. John draws this face of Jesus with poignant detail.

> I know your works [says Jesus]: you are neither cold nor hot. Would that you were either cold or hot! So, because you are lukewarm, and neither hot nor cold, I will spit you out of my mouth. For you say, I am rich, I have prospered, and I need nothing, not realizing that you are wretched, pitiable, poor, blind, and naked. I counsel you to buy from me gold refined by fire… Those whom I love, I reprove and discipline, so be zealous and repent.⁴¹

My primary experience of God is as a friend who loves me with sweet kisses, me and those affected by my business. But I've seen His other face, too, and know that in His hand is a rod applied when I stray too far or too long from Truth. There is never the Friend without the Lord or the Lord without the Friend. How could it be otherwise when great power, holiness, and mercy meet us? How else could He walk with us in the midst of our ignorant arrogance or our terror-filled nights? He knows our limits and is mostly loving in the way we expect loving to show up. He continually provides good, goods, and other goodnesses. Such anyway is my experience. Jesus is Friend and Lord, Truth and Love, power and gentleness in one.

---

⁴⁰Revelation 6:15-17 NCV
⁴¹Revelation 3: 15-21 ESV

God calls. God wants a relationship with you. He has been there on the other side all along, knocking at the door of your heart; will you knock at His? Will you ask to enter His heart and for His heart to live in you?

I Knocked, He Opened, Now What?

Did you knock? Did He open? Did you step over the threshold from disbelief to belief? From distrust to trust? Close the door behind you, latch it. Walk in. The old you is history; leave it for the historians. Walk on.

God is alive in you, and you are alive in God. You have the prize. The prize is a relationship with Almighty God, Prince of Peace, Eternal Father, Source of Sustenance, Jewel of Joy. What wonder! What life! Nothing compares. And nothing is more foundational to your organizational good than what you just did. Rejoice in the freedom.

For some, the clouds part, trumpets trumpet, violins harmonize, and in a moment all looks different. For most, a new way daily dawns, as a rising sun warming crops growing in the field. Suddenly or steadily, you are changed. It is done.

A new road stretches out before you, wither it goes is between you and God. When you are ready, turn the page and start a new life of leadership. We're going surfing.

Chapter Eight

WAVE

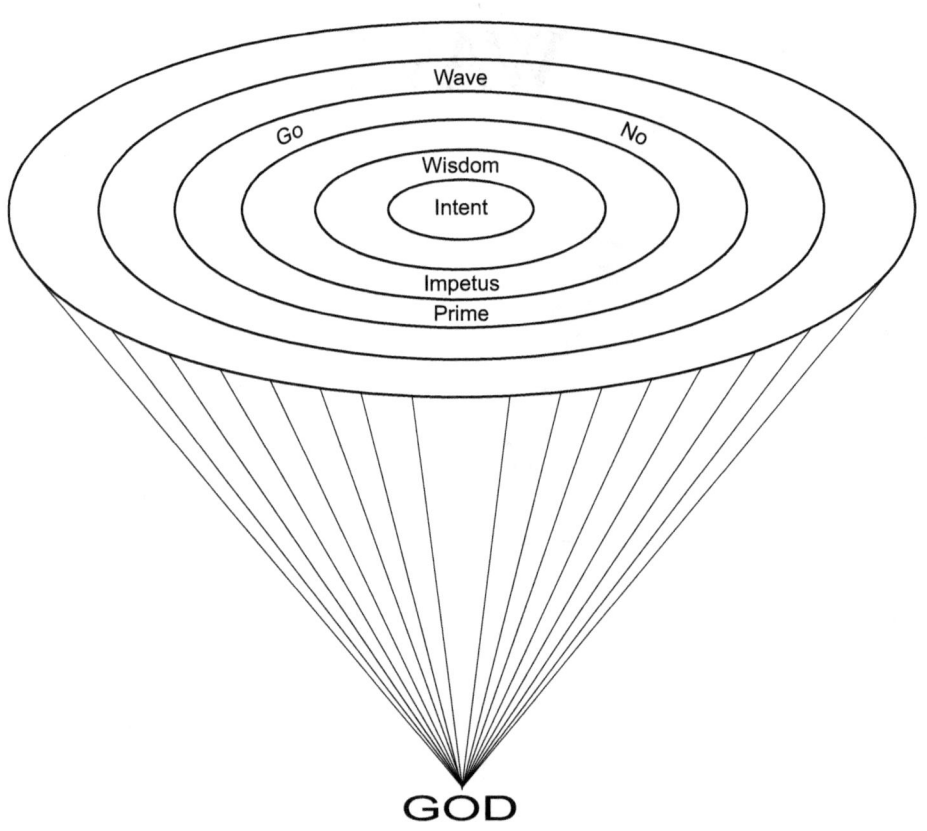

*The horse is prepared for the day of
battle, but victory belongs to the Lord.*

Proverbs 21:31
(NASB)

Now we get down to business—God's business. The following four modes are about resting while active, for His yoke is easy, and His burden is light.[42] Four hands on the wheel, not two; you relax your grip and trust. Working with God, He moves and you move with Him. Soul effort is released, and yet life is good and right. You realize you never owned your life anyway; it has always been God's graced gift.

The rest of this book is about how to be the new CEO, the Chief's Executive Officer, daily. Not that you'll be perfect: you don't *achieve* perfection working with God; you relax into it, into Him, and He develops you into His CEO.

Regardless of whether you ran into God's house or stepped cautiously over the threshold, you gave God control over your life. Now God can lift you on a wave, moving you from Point A to Point B, and your soul won't pop back to live in No mode, even if at work you still access No.

Where do you go? Where God goes. When do you go? When God goes. With whom do you go? With whom God says to or arranges for you to go. What do you do? What God directs you to do. Why these? Because God is with you to do this, and God is God, and who are you? He Will Be What He Will Be. Therefore, success is His. Once you get the hang of this, it is deeply restful. Inside, you and your

---

[42] For those not familiar with New Testament jargon, a light yoke refers to the agricultural practice of harnessing two oxen together to pull a plow in tandem, that is, to work hard. Oxen yokes were, like the oxen, heavy. In a parable, Jesus asks the hearer to imagine himself yoked to one of those oxen, having to bear the burden of a heavy workload, then imagine themselves working with him instead: "Come to me, all who labor and are heavy laden, and I will give you rest. Take *my* yoke upon you, and learn from *me*, for I am gentle and lowly in heart, and you will find rest for your souls. 30 For my yoke is easy, and my burden is light." (Matthew 11:28-30 ESV—author's italics.)

soul rest in God's direction, God's leadership. Outside, you ride the waves. As best you can, of course, we're still prone to make mistakes. That's okay; God usually rolls more than one wave your way.

Having given God control of your life circumstances, you will have the dedication, lightness, and flexibility needed to surf. Your circumstances may begin to show greater success or failure as the world around you defines them. But beyond ups and downs, the win is interacting with God at the crest of a wave and bringing new life to your organization. Here, then, is your new definition of success: time lived with God.

Some people liken God in His infiniteness to the seas. Infinite is a bit bigger than the Pacific, but let's explore the variety and richness of how Wave operates. We'll do that by joining a few executives as they surf.

Mark's Story, (Completed)

We last left Mark Whitacre in Chapter Five, literally imprisoned in "No" mode. There he sat, barred from any accomplishment that people on the outside would have seen as a success. But painful as they were, Mark is grateful for those years. He sees the success in them.

Before prison, Mark did not believe that God was real. He, therefore, naturally thought that unless he himself was unceasingly diligent in arranging his circumstances, his life was not going to be satisfactory. Out of that anxiety, he tried to ride a wave that was too big for him, too big for anyone's soul, a wave of money, with the surfboard of embezzling. When the wave crashed, so did he. He attempted suicide. His family was fractured. His organization's reputation suffered.

God Waves. But as they say, God sends the cure before the disease. God waved at Mark, calling out a sweet hello. In the first wave, God saves Mark from death and then sends a fellow scientist to talk to him about God. In the midst of condemnation, Mark had a friend.

With Mark now in prison, God rolls Mark a second wave: He sends him a new friend to talk with. Mark's eyes open; he gives control of his circumstances, sorrows, pains, and potential to God. Mark sought and knocked. Jesus opened the door, and a wave of internal change pulled Mark through into God's business. Before the second wave, he had a love for himself and his extensions (family, status, possessions); now, he simply had love. Instead of seeing only himself and what had been taken from him, he could now see others and see them with love. He saw opportunities to give.

With a third wave God lifted Mark up and carried him in a new direction. The man who earned three higher education degrees was now helping other inmates get their GED. He was no longer living for himself. Though living in prison, internally, he was free.

Even if internally free, however, prison is still severely challenging. According to a study cited by Florida State University's criminologists, each year of incarceration increases the chances by an average of 32 percent that an inmate will divorce.[43] Most with more than five years in prison leave divorced. Mark was sentenced to nine years.

Mark's inner house restored and sentence eventually served, God sent a fourth wave: Mark's wife Ginger had

---

[43]Siennick, Sonja E.; Stewart, Eric A.; & Staff, Jeremy (2014). Explaining the association between incarceration and divorce. *Criminology*. vol. 52 (3) pp. 371-398

waited, and his family gave him a second chance. God's wave lifted Mark up out of his prison of aloneness and anxiety to place him down in togetherness, security, and freedom under God and His perfect plans.

And finally, the fifth wave: almost immediately upon his release, a biotech firm recruited Mark as COO. Considering his past, that was a miracle. While it is God's wave and to Him the praise is due, Cypress Systems Inc. and President Paul A. Willis deserve kudos for risking their reputation. Their statement revealed the extent of Mark's restoration:

> We are fully aware of the details of this case and Dr. Whitacre's specific involvement. We consider ourselves to be among a growing list of supporters, which include current and former FBI agents, former U.S. and Canadian prosecutors, several prominent law firms, and numerous other professionals. We desire, like others, to move forward from this point and build a positive contribution in several health-related research areas. Mark Whitacre will be a valued asset in that ongoing effort.[44]

Each wave lifted Mark higher. He went from prison cell to family man and COO in 60 seconds. That's mental-emotional whiplash. But Mark's solid spiritual core gave him the agility to surf the waves. God continued waving Mark forward. For a while, Mark was even COO of two not-small organizations simultaneously. Surfing God's waves, he has moved the lives of thousands. Mark managed staff and

---

[44] https://www.biospace.com/article/releases/-b-mark-whitacre-ph-d-b-joins-management-team-at-b-cypress-systems-inc-b-/

projects in Prime. He also became an ethics evangelist. His life became of God, by God, and for God. God and Mark continue to leave a powerful wake together.

Wave Defined

Wave is where God opens opportunities for change to happen in a moment. Lighter yet more powerful than *Go*, Wave is the mode in which God's victorious *YES* reaches out from eternity to move you and your organization. It quantitatively and/or qualitatively changes your company's reality. It lifts you up and sets you down on a new shore where you and your organization are perfectly placed to fulfill your mission and change one piece of the world in a way that also advances His other purposes. And you get to be a key part of that. Your actions in *Go* were as a slow shadow; in Wave, you move lightly and quickly with the power of God's intent, impetus, and wisdom. Speed happens when we are present and do not get in the way of God's plans; instead, we execute them.

> *That which happens in an instant in Wave, you and God work out over time in our world through the first six modes.*

When you sign your first contract with Amazon to distribute goods or with a national grocery chain to provide labeled products, your business life is instantly in a new reality. You ride the crest of the wave that God sent you. In Prime, you manage marketing, supply, finance, and/or those who do. They are the surfboards with which you surf the waves. That which happens in an instant in Wave, you and God work out over time in our world through the first six modes.

Challenge. Wave challenges your innate desire to control. In Wave, we give up control *now*. If we don't, we miss the wave or get knocked over by trying to redirect it. You can't overpower an ocean wave and make it go where it isn't going. Rather, you work *with* its power. Same with God's wave. You choose whether to catch a wave in a life-filled instant that shows whether you are ready to give God control in this next opportunity. That particular wave will never come again. A different wave may bring you to a different shore at a different time; you can serve there, too. But life in Wave is *this* wave surfed now, or with discernment wisely avoided because the opportunity was for you to master your ego by avoiding the external opportunity.

Training for correct loss of control that you will encounter in Wave is one reason you call on God throughout your journey in the first six modes. Learning risky obedience is unlikely if you don't practice with the small changes first. In your first round of *Go*, you own the business. In Wave, you are a managing partner. He is the owner and Chair (or Throne). With practice, when you spot a God-wave, your body, mind, policy, communications, and resource allocation all jump onto your surfboard to catch His wave. Practicing partnering with God in the first six modes trains us to handle change through submission to His will.

Just ask Kurt. Or Jim.

Kurt's Story (continued)

In the previous chapter, we saw SVP Kurt surrender his self-driven career in the commercial side of outer space.

That required surrendering his inner-space commitment to never quitting. 'Surrender' isn't 'quitting'; he transferred controlling ownership of his career and life to God. That's trusting. And it changed Kurt's relationship with God. It allowed God to give Kurt a whole new vista. As soon as Kurt surrendered control, God lifted him up on a wave.

Instead of letting Kurt go, his CEO transitioned him to Senior Commercial Advisor. In that role, he could access the special talents that he had been gaining over the years. He became an advisor, mentor, and sage. With the major hurdle of humility passed God's wave was able to carry him to what God esteemed, not what Kurt's self-image demanded. God didn't need Kurt to spend life holding the don't-be-a-quitter gauntlet he picked up as a child.

God now needed Kurt to use his love and wisdom to teach and uplift others, to make them more effective, empowered, and balanced. Now, along with providing guidance on situations around global sales and 5G spectrum policy, Kurt also advised and coached the very executives at Intelsat who could have lost respect for him for giving up. Instead, his going through the door increased their respect. How's Kurt? To say "happier" is to understate; he is renewed, bigger, with more room in his heart and more life in his life. He operates with less internal resistance. He has more family time, more community time, and more study time. Rather than his time supporting his income, his income supports his time.

Kurt's reduced resistance let Intelsat try other sales and marketing options. Those options did not bring the desired results either; the company saw that it needed to restructure. When Kurt made the decision to let go with God, the wave quickly crested, carrying the company to new good.

That new good was the qualitative *more* that his soul and organization needed.

Jim's Story, and Instructions for Surfing

Four years after founding the analytics firm Tiber Solutions, CEO Jim Hadley caught a wave. A VP in a firm larger than Tiber subcontracted Tiber to fulfill a data analytics contract to a third, even larger, company. The VP was subcontracting Jim's whole team. God waved at Jim. When the VP's CEO came back from leave, however, she nixed Jim's employees, allowing only Jim to stay on contract. When the wave arrived, it was smaller than when it was farther out. It was a roll, a small swell. Even-keeled and grateful to God for His provisions, CEO Jim served solo there for two and a half years as he kept his own employees busy on projects elsewhere. Jim swam the swell with grace.

Surf Skill #1: Humility. Whether we notice or miss them, God's waves typically start small. If you want to catch a God wave, keep your eye on the small waves and treat them with the respect due to anything that comes from God. Match the small waves with a humble attitude. Jim did. He displayed the first quality a person needs to ride God's Wave: humility. We practice humility in Prime; in Wave, we solidify it as there is no question that we stand in front of God. If God offers a small contract, recognize its source and treat it with the consideration and respect due to the One who sent it your way. Whether you pursue it is a technical question answered in Prime, but listen and see; don't let business analytics decide for you that you should disregard a small wave. God's business is pursued God's way, with humility.

Jim's humility showed up daily through diligence, quality, and commitment. He had allowed himself to be an individual contributor. The subcontracting gig was over, and Jim was back focusing on being Tiber's CEO. Several years roll by. Then, God sends another wave. Jim relates:

> One of the employees of this company I had worked with in partnership—we were a good team together—after I left, she just continued to be successful, being promoted, promoted, promoted to the point where she became the deputy CIO. And she called me and said, "We're going to give you guys a sole source contract because we're ready for analytics, and we really want to do this." And she introduced me to some of the people on the business side in leadership, some of the Vice Presidents over there, and God just blessed those communications. They understood my approach, and they liked the fact that I had been in this organization for two and a half years, so I knew the lingo, I knew the business. They [did not trust people] on the IT side, anybody technology-wise, but for some reason, God blessed that relationship and they said, "Yeah, let's bring on a team of 4 people, let's start going."

Surf Skill #2: Strength. New wave, new qualities used by the surfer. This time, Tiber was hired directly, not through an intermediary. Jim's new wave is now four times larger. Four times the mass in motion is four times the impetus to manage and four times the risk. To accomplish this, he needed strength, which included focus, alertness, willingness, and faith. The first little wave involved him mostly in Go; this surfing demanded the full balancing act of Prime, which synthesizes all previous modes, plus making sure to stay surrendered and on this side of the door.

Jim managed his people and the project well, and the wave built momentum. Jim again:

> That team was successful, and after about three months with that group, I added another team of four people, and then they said they wanted a third team of four people. Ultimately, we had 14 people on that account.

Within a year of this new wave reaching Jim, Tiber Solutions had more than doubled. They went from 10 people to 26. That is Wave, and to surf, Jim had to develop his strength in Prime. That included building a network. Of course, God, walking with you in relationship, knows how flexible, capable, and connected you are and aren't. He deals with your capacity in one of His sweetest ways: perfect timing.

Surf Skill #3: Keeping Heaven's Time. Jim continues:

> Just because they wanted me to bring on a third team doesn't mean I *can*. I'd like to, but I have to find four qualified people who don't grow on trees. So [Jim looks up to indicate praying], "Lord, I know you don't want me to compromise in who I am hiring; I'm not going to just bring on anybody, so, alright, Lord."

> So He started providing these people. People who were already working for me [told me about] one of their friends they worked with for 10 years and is now

out of work. Perfect timing. I go talk to them, great fit. Humble, confident, lifelong learner, great technologist, loyal, dedicated, worker, servant heart. That person is a gem, and that person the Lord provided. So then these other three people kind of show up to round out a team of four. That's God's confirmation.

If she had told me to bring on three teams Day One, I would have bowed out. Yes, it's money, but I want it to go well. God needed to prepare my heart too, to grow the company to that size.

From the start, Jim's humility allowed him to see God as the one he serves, not vice versa. Jim stayed in *Go* and *No* at the right times and with the right intensity to surf a succession of perfectly paced waves. God lifted Jim up from who he was to who he had to become to surf the wave that more than doubled his company. Along the way, *God* lifted all boats.

Surf Skill #4: Victory. We love success stories. But don't confuse success with victory. We don't control success. We can influence it, but it comes and goes despite our best efforts. In Wave, however, there is victory over failure *and* over success. Through Wave, God brings you beyond success and failure.

Waves don't stay at the crest-stage; waves move you to a new shore where they fall, are pulled back into the ocean, and leave you in a new place. Success appears during the wave's build-up and crest stages; victory happens when you trust God rather than the particular wave. Trusting God leaves very minimal disorientation when the wave disappears. God is behind each mode, including Wave. You don't move from God; you just recognize when it is time to change mode. After the wave leaves you on a new shore, that may mean heading straight into Go to produce new services for a new market. Or it may mean that you need a whole new intent (in Intent), or a new strategic forecast and plan (Wisdom), or just to stop expanding (No). Or some combination of the above.

Four months after Jim first told me his story, I circled back around. Things were different now. A new CIO had come in who would only work with analytics vendors with $100M+ revenue. It wasn't pretty: Jim had 14 people working there, and the company gave him six days' notice. The wave crashed quickly.

Jim, however, did not crash. He stood on a new shore and relied on his relationship with God just as he had relied on that relationship to surf the wave. He prayed his worry to God about how he was going to care for all the people he had to let go.

By this point in his life, Jim had practiced discernment enough to understand God's reply. Jim recounts God's counsel: "God said: 'What are you talking about? They are My people; I take care of them. No worry.'" Jim now had the strength to prioritize his employees' transitions. Within a month, God, through Jim, and Jim, through God, had helped half of Tiber's staff find employment elsewhere.

Jim endured pain and loss but stayed in victory for himself and others by continuing to work with God. In Wave, Jim was lifted beyond success and failure; Jim was in victory. As previously mentioned, God's business seems backward. But anyone who risks is eventually crestfallen. What, or who, you focus on when you fall, determines how long the broken bones stay broken and how fast you get up. To strengthen your leadership, focus on the One who never falls.

And count your blessings.

Chapter Nine

HARVEST

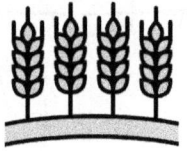

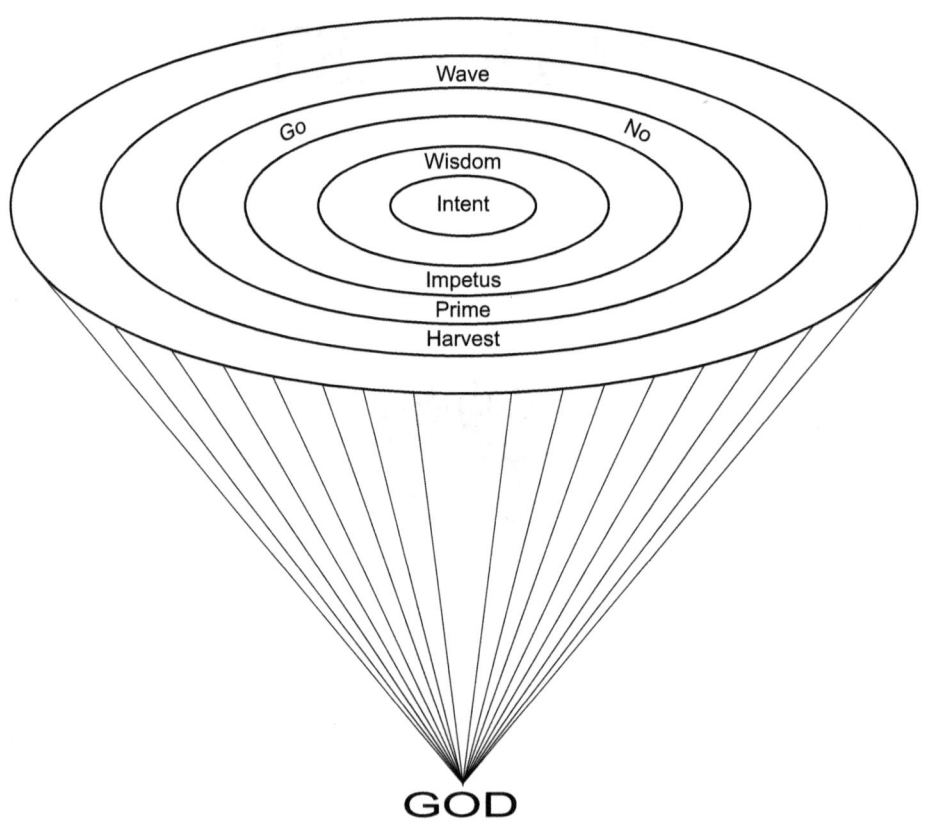

And they came to Bethlehem at the beginning of barley harvest... So she gleaned in the field until evening... Then Naomi her mother-in-law said to her, "My daughter, should I not seek rest for you, that it may be well with you?

Ruth 1:22; 2:17; 3:1
(ESV)

After a long day surfing waves, after a long quarter building results, it's time to come home and feast on the generated bounty. It's Harvest time.

By this point in your working with God, you see God doing things in your life and your business. It has seeped in that God ongoingly gives you that life and business and, therefore, that your life is not completely your own. You live, experience, and have opinions about it, but you can't control it and stop it from being taken from you at some point. We don't own our position or even own our life; we just rent them for a while and then they're gone. How can we handle this discomforting idea? We've found a bigger love.

Under the powerful name of Jehovah (YHVH), God, Beloved, Jesus, we are led, protected, provided for, and drawn out beyond ourselves. As we granted Him permission in going through a door, and solidified that permission by getting on a metaphoric surfboard, He established in us a qualitatively more abundant relationship with the world. Realizing that with God all things are possible, you now have a relationship of wonder and appreciation. Aligned with His will, we've become useful in ways we probably never guessed. We've become fragrant. We are His harvest, and He and His glory are our bounty.

Harvest Defined

Harvest is the space in which, freed from the burden of government of the self by the self and for the self, we regain youthful joy. In Harvest, we rejoice. We rejoice over success but also in failure. We rejoice because God is with us. Life is in us and around us. No matter what. And because we know that we are in God's business and God is ours, we also now have peace. "Peace, love, and joy," it sounds so 1960s, I know. But this is the matured version of 'tune in, turn on, and drop out.' Tuning into God's workings, we've turned on to working with God and dropped out of the heavy belief that the burden is on us always to work harder and deliver better, faster, and more. And though we feel less burdened, we've taken increased responsibility for ourselves and others—a God-oriented community sprouts around us.

Harvest is internal and external bounty. In Harvest, the two meanings of "appreciation" unite. Growth and internal enrichment increase. Even if the less likely option of losing everything happens in Wave, we accumulate internal strength by rising above the crash, in love with God all the more for showing us Truth that surpasses achievement or loss. In Harvest, we gather that increase. We stop for a moment, count it, *appreciate it*, and rest in gratitude and enjoy it—a most capital appreciation!

Harvest characteristic #1: Filled up. In Harvest, we feel no lack. We feel God's provision's fulness and the moment's radiant specialness with Him. The green pastures and still waters King David mentions in Psalm 23 are accessed in Harvest mode. As with the No mode, we don't seek an increase. But whereas in No, we put forth effort to stop growth, in Harvest, we are actually satisfied, even abundantly full. The desired outcome is here. We are not pushing forward, neither are we pushing back, nor are we stagnating. We experience fullness.

If your company has investors or stockholders, it is important that they enter the internal harvest with you, otherwise they may draw you back into "*Go*" before you have completely reaped the bounty of broadened perspective that you get in Harvest. We experience the fullness of God's bounty on five levels:

1. Physical (healthy structure and finances, stakeholders receiving increased value)
2. Emotional (joy; clear communication; synergy)
3. Mental (positive perceptions, clarity, orderliness, fresh creativity)
4. Social (positive community)
5. Spiritual (God's business is being done; He is with you, and you know it)

Your organization can harvest each level of bounty because you led your team wisely through the waves. God was with you and still is. Mark didn't get himself hired as a COO straight out of prison, Karl didn't plan to get Intelsat reorganized, and Jim didn't time his client's requests so he could add more teams. These executives led themselves and their organizations to increased bounty by being with God and letting God lead them.

Action Steps

1. Examine your organization at each of the five levels of bounty listed above. If you don't have an organization at the moment, examine your own life. Note areas of abundance and of lack.
2. Pinpoint the origin of any lack by unit, managerial level, and mode.
3. Discern if the lack is due to a temporary circumstance or a chronic blockage. If it is due to a chronic blockage, the organization in that area is likely relying on itself without God. Find out first if there is a parallel

blockage in yourself. If there is, dismantle your dam and hand the debris to God. Then, deal with the organizational blockage right now if possible; if not, then at the appropriate time(s).

Harvest characteristic #2: No drama. Awake and operating, we go about without drama, without games. There is zero drama because we aren't driven by fear. We see that God provides. Just as we can experience peace and bounty in the seventh day (Sabbath), we can access peace and bounty in this seventh mode (Harvest). In Harvest, we can rest.

Non-Action Questions

1. What place does rest have in your organization?
2. Where does your team experience include rest?
3. Does the team manager have a core of trust or distrust inside herself?

Harvest characteristic #3: Gratitude. An organization in Harvest mode still has the honesty and humility that characterize Prime culture and the humble possibilitarianism that characterizes Wave culture. Harvest then adds recognition and celebration to the group culture. Recognition and celebration stem from gratitude. You can't experience Harvest without experiencing gratitude. The infusion of gratitude in Harvest creates a culture of listening where new ideas are heard and treated with respect.

Workship. As a leader in Harvest, you are clear about the source of the bounty. Your gratitude is not showered only on your people; you also thank God. And when your joy touches gratitude, it combines naturally into worship.

Thank God. Your work becomes devotional. It becomes "workship." Maybe your grateful, prayerful, attitude spreads. You hire a chaplain or set of chaplains to facilitate thanks and prayers to God at work. However it happens, heaven hears, and God responds with love: workship moves your company forward.

Jubilant gratitude. The Hebrew for "harvest," synonymous in the Hebrew Bible with the noun "yield," is *yevul*. A slightly different form of the root word *yvl* describes what happens after seven cycles of seven harvests: *yovel*. *Yovel* is typically translated as "jubilee." In the Bible, the jubilee was the year in which people were freed up from indentured servitude, rested, and lived on the bounty of previous years instead of toiling in the fields. Now, it commonly means 'celebration.' In Harvest, there is always room for jubilant celebrations and daily gratitude.

> **Action Question**
>
> Layered on top of your Prime culture of honesty and humility, how much of Wave's possibilitarianism and Harvest's culture of recognition and celebration does your organization, team, or project have?

Harvest characteristic #4: Glory. You gave celebratory, even jubilant, thanks to God. That means you had a glimpse of the wondrousness of God. In a virtuous cycle of giving, God responds by providing you and your people with increased wonder and a sense of His glory. The Harvest isn't full without experiencing God's glory. As that happens, we get even smaller, and He gets even bigger in our life. Some organizations have the shadow reflections of glory: power and excitement. They have 'that something special in the air.'

But it's about them. Some organizations have beauty, but God's glory is more than human grace or beauty. When you also have humility, love for others, trust in God, and peace, you are ripe to see God's glory.

Clearly, Harvest is the place to be. Harvest also holds up a high bar beyond the current state of many, if not most, organizations. Our idea of a harvest is mainly limited to a financial windfall. But Harvest demands that we get beyond the American ethic of individualism. At the same time, we must avoid a pendulum swing into caring too much about what others say and following the latest fads. Being positive, grateful, loving, and celebratory doesn't mean we should lose the perspective of grounded wisdom. It's just that our wisdom expands to better include God as the prime context of goodness.

> *Provision comes from God.*

In Harvest, we see that our provision comes from God. There is encouragement of individual and group success but not adulation of it; neither do we seek to blame. We see that we are wonderful, but only because we are His creation and care. We've been through No, so we're honest about our limitations. We're not self-important—all the more reason to be thankful for our success and for opportunities to grow from our mistakes. We think: glory to God. For from Him the glory arrives.

Action Question

What simple steps are you taking in your organization to turn focus away from egos, even from the collective 'power of us,' to elevate the Source of all provision?

Harvest: no drama, bounty, gratitude, glory. How does it happen? Not easily. Let's continue a paused CEO story to see how he found rest in Harvest.

Jeff's Story, Continued

When we last left Jeff Skeen in Intent, he was fresh out of college and on his way to fulfilling his intent to be the CEO of a publicly traded company. However, he couldn't shake the widow's offer. Taking advice from his father, he chose to give the hardware store turnaround his best shot. He left the sexy $70K+ corporate job opportunity for $19K and hard work in hardware.

Go and No. Day after very long day, Jeff diligently applied himself to the business. He hardly saw friends and stopped going to church. He was destined to be the CEO of a publicly traded company, a huge undertaking that demanded complete focus and dedication.

"About a year and a half into the business," says Jeff, "I started losing weight. I didn't feel very good; I wouldn't eat. My wife was like: 'I think you need to go to the doctor.' Well, as a man, I don't go to the doctor… 'It's indigestion; it'll be fine'," Jeff said. Resting was not a priority; the hard work and long nights paid off. In just a few years, he turned around the store's finances and sold it.

During the sale of the company, one of the bankers asked if he wanted to take over an IT operation. Cha-ching! Again, he applied himself. He knew nothing about computers, but he could learn. He read vociferously. At home, at night and on the weekends, you could find Jeff taking apart computer hardware to figure out its workings. Even though he and his wife were living in a small townhouse, they hardly saw each other; he was dedicated to becoming a success. He was disciplined; he was an athlete. He could do it.

The Door. Straying from Wisdom, he kept losing weight. The doctor found that he did not have cancer, just a much less dramatic and more easily curable condition. "I'm not a psychiatrist," said the doctor, "but I believe you have occupational depression." Many people would be relieved at the non-cancer diagnosis. But not Jeff. "This may sound really weird," he said, "I wish he would have said I had cancer." When we hit a crisis, we reveal our core motivators. For Jeff, it was control. "Cancer was something out of my control," he explained, "and in my mind, depression was in my control. I had a military family; I was an athlete; I couldn't have depression; that was for the weak." It didn't compute that there was something in his life that he should be able to control but couldn't. He had to succeed.

Jeff had burned himself out. He asked the doctor for a pill so he could get back to work. The doctor said no. "What are you recommending?" Jeff inquired. "Quit your job," the doctor responded. "I couldn't quit," Jeff told himself. "I'd never quit anything." He went home. His wife listened. Then she, too, told him to quit.

Jeff had overvalued doing (*Go*) and discipline (*No*). He couldn't allow himself to recognize his own needs, which were as plain as day to his wife and his doctor. He hadn't noticed when reliance on self-discipline became an altar on which he was sacrificing himself to please the God of success that was making Jeff over in its image: CEO of a publicly traded company. And we thought Baal was only biblical. ("Baal," by the way, means "master.") Someplace in his soul, though, he knew what his doctor and wife knew: his God of success wasn't enough. They knew that for Jeff to be whole, he had to do a Gideon and knock the God of success off the altar of self-discipline. Gaining wisdom can cost a dream.

"I can't quit now," he said. "I've been planning since childhood to become the CEO of a publicly traded company. These are the plans that my father and I have been working on my whole life." Nevertheless, trusting doctor, wife, and that small voice by which his soul spoke, Jeff called on his discipline to undo his reliance on discipline. He achieved one last achievement: he quit.

Jeff said: "That was the sweetest time of my life. I would never trade in that depression for anything." Why? Anyone who has emerged victorious from a crisis understands that sometimes we have to have our smaller treasures taken so we can find bigger ones. Depressed, with no job and no direction, he prayed.

And God answered. God highlighted a couple of Bible passages for Jeff. They shifted Jeff's perspective and awakened in him new life. When Jesus seemed to be talking to his disciples, Jeff knew that Jesus was talking directly to him.

> Therefore I tell you, do not be anxious about your life, what you will eat, nor about your body, what you will put on. For life is more than food, and the body more than clothing. Consider the ravens: they neither sow nor reap, they have neither storehouse nor barn, and yet God feeds them. Of how much more value are you than the birds! And which of you by being anxious can add a single hour to his span of life? ... Do not seek what you are to eat and what you are to drink, nor be worried... Instead, seek his kingdom, and these things will be added to you.[45]

---

[45] Luke 12:22-31 (ESV)

In Jeff's words: "What I realized was that the goal I was setting for my life was too small. I wasn't seeking the kingdom [of God]." Jeff's horizon got much broader. He understood why he was depressed: he was constricting his soul. The constriction had blinded his eyes to the glory of God's kingdom. He began to find worth in moments where God peeked through the clouds, what he would call 'kingdom moments.'

Jeff told God that he would do whatever God wanted. Forget CEO; he'd flip burgers and mop floors. Being with God was far better than being alone and stressed. He had found unshakeable love and great glory. He'd found The Door and knocked.

Wave. Right on cue, God sent Jeff a wave of interviews with good companies. He was back on track.

Fabulous. Still, approach bounty with caution: if this is you getting back on track, you must ask: onto whose track am I putting my train: God's or mine? As was the perfume offer, these interviews were the kind of test that God sometimes throws our way to help us discover for ourselves who we are and where we live. Were these offers leading just to more *Go*, or were they a wave of offers from God that would be treated as a Wave offering by Jeff back to God?[46]

While Jeff's interviews for "high-powered jobs" were happening, a few high school buddies invited him to partner in owning and running a small Gold's Gym franchise

---

[46] As Biblically prescribed, ancient Israelites gave different 'offerings' to God. One of these was a 'wave offering' where the offeror waved his donated meat and grain in the direction of heaven, then burned it on the altar to provide a pleasing aroma to God. Translated to today, that would be donating money or time to please God. We typically see a job offer as being for us to benefit us. But in God's kingdom, job offers, like so much else, are reversed: we offer our job and a portion of its harvest back to God.

in a small town 45 minutes away. For Jeff, that was back to the bottom. Jeff turned to God: "I told You I would do anything. But to work at a gym?? Are you kidding me? We have a treadmill; it's a little gym; this is really going to be the death of my entire career." God calmly reminded him of his love-filled declaration to serve and told him this was his chance. But pride is a squirrelly thing. Jeff knew his wife would tell him to turn down his buddies' small-time vision, so to have an excuse to get back to his shiny career prospects, he asked her if he should take the offer.

He was looking outward from his soul, seeing big things and wanting them for himself. He was looking out for results as far as he could see, which to him wasn't far since he was only looking at the walls of a small gym. But God is smarter. His wife told him to take the offer, to go have some fun with his buddies at the gym. *Surprise!* She had God's perspective.

His wife was looking into his eternal soul and wanted what would make his soul happy and healthy. And that was not going to be another race to the top. Sufficiently aware of God's ways, Jeff saw God working in his wife. Jeff said yes to the right thing, no to the wrong thing. He was back in Wisdom-filled Prime mode. Jeff popped his self-important image as CEO of a publicly traded company. Instead, he settled for co-owner of a treadmill. He was surfing God's wave, even if it was only a slight swell.

Then God lifted Jeff up with wave after wave of success. One gym became eleven. With 40% corporate EBITDA[47], the partners had the most profitable Gold's Gym chain in the world. They raised capital and bought the entire company.

---

[47] Earnings Before Interest Taxes Depreciation and Amortization

Harvest. Does Jeff say, "I built that"? He puts it this way: "That was God's doing. I [only] worked as hard as everybody else [no more]. And probably not half as smart as [others]. He turned that into a great career for me." Jeff is grateful. Sometimes, God sends people to cross Jeff's path, people who hold little or no career purpose for him. Jeff stops, sees, invites them out to lunch, listens, and celebrates their accomplishments. He has eyes of abundance and humility. Jeff reaped a huge harvest. Money isn't the main point; however, the money is the pointer.

Now, years later, having sold Gold's Gym and reached about $1B in fitness and healthcare transactions, Jeff has spent his years providing people the opportunity to be exactly what he wasn't until he let God get hold of him: healthy. Physically (he gained the weight back), emotionally (raised up out of depression), mentally (likewise, not depressed but humble and hopeful), socially (not lonely), spiritually (he lives in a relationship with God and spreads God and His goodness in multiple ways). With all that success, CEO Jeff is clear on how to access God's bounty and rest: choose Jesus, choose victory over success, and live obediently and gratefully in a relationship with God. He puts it this way: "This is why I exist: to serve God... I have the blessing of truly serving the kingdom [of God]. I got to tell you: it's awesome knowing there's God in control."

As we say in Harvest: *hallelujah*.

CHAPTER TEN

DEATH

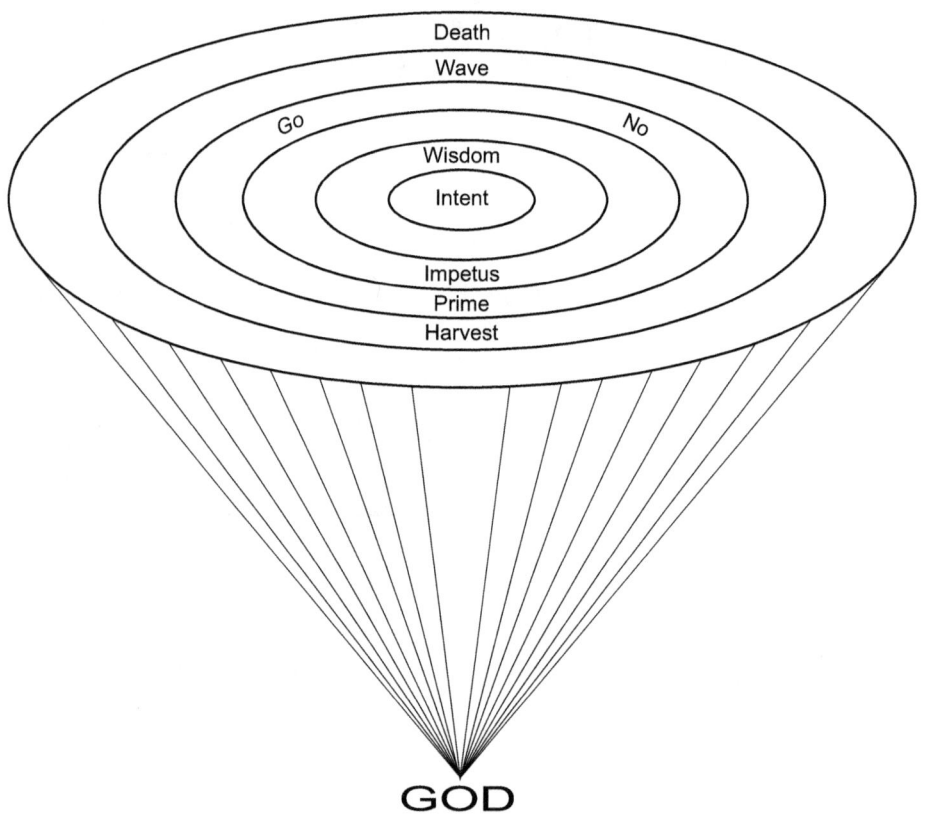

After these things God tested Abraham and said to him, "Abraham!"

And he said, "Here I am."

Then He said, "Take your son, your only son Isaac, whom you love, and go to the land of Moriah, and offer him there as a burnt offering on one of the mountains of which I will tell you."

So Abraham rose up early in the morning and saddled his donkey, and took two of his young men with him and Isaac his son; and he split the wood for the burnt offering, and arose and went to the place that God had told him.

Genesis 22:1-3
(MEV)

In Wave, we started to participate in meaningful co-creation with God, with more ease, in His business.[48] We become possibilitarians as our world changes. In Harvest, we live in the ease and bounteousness of God's Harvest. We have peace, inner strength, abundance, and gratitude. All this while maintaining or growing an organization that adds value to others, transitions it to the next generation, and gives gratitude to God. We have arrived at completion.

Or so it feels. Harvest mode may be your best friend for quite a while. Bringing your organization into Harvest mode is a worthwhile use of time. Harvest is restful, satisfying, and wonderous. And it puts you in a united, mutually supportive, God community.

Indeed, some will stay in these eight modes: Intent through Harvest. That will be wonderful. And still, some souls yearn for something more, something undefined. Once we are through the Door and into His business, God gives us more hunger, too.

You don't want two businesses anymore. You feel the constriction of working your own business, almost the dirtiness. You only want to be part of God's business. Whatever happens to your organization or your family, they also belong to God. Eventually, we say, 'God, Harvest mode is fabulous, but I need more of You.' God replies: 'Human, give me more of *you*.'

One day, your body will be laid to rest, other leaders will take your place and do well (or not), and your children and grandchildren will move on. Leaning into that pre-mortem, ask yourself: Where is my truest home: where am I *fully* alive now?

---

[48]The concept of co-creation should be treated carefully. Only God truly creates; however, together we re-form our house from the material He created.

You have to answer that for yourself, of course. But chew on this: God is in you right here, right now. His ever-present self is home. The question is: how do you stay in your ultimate home while being out in the workplace? As you might guess by the title of this chapter, the next step is a doozy.

Death Defined

"Death" is surrendering personal identity to live with God. Ultimately, we are either a vehicle for God (I-Will-Be-What-I-Will-Be) or for identity (I will be whatever my personal "I" tells me I must be). When God tells you that He wants more of you, He is not saying you should try harder, do more good, or be better. That is worth repeating: when God tells you that He wants more of you, He is not saying that you should try harder, do more good, or be a better person. He simply asks us to adopt His will, His *living* will, in every situation. Simple, but oh, such a challenge to pride and ego. He drops the bar so low that only the dead can cross under it.

Being dead is not *not* having any desire. It is where no desires but the desires of God have you. Here you are free. The purpose of the mode of Death is to leave you with only one desire: living with God.

> *"Death" is surrendering personal identity to live with God.*

To be sure, Death is a difficult mode. If you contract with God to put a hit out on your identity, if you tell God that all you want is Him and actually mean it, He will do it. A good bit of it won't be pleasant. But it will be good.

As far as lies, illusions, manipulations, fears, and anything self-aggrandizing can go with you on this journey through the modes, they can't survive a complete trip through Death mode. God may ask you to stop the campaign that your new CMO just told you about, the one that is launching this afternoon, the one that tells all the right people about how great your organization is, how it is the perfect solution to (_name of customer problem_), the one that markets a solution that 'by chance' you just found out is based on something ridiculously close to your competitor's copyrighted IP. And according to the contract, you'll already have to pay the subcontractors regardless of whether the campaign launches.

Death mode is a major league play for those who want God. And, given enough time, God always wins. But remember, it is for the good. I'm serious about that, not sarcastic. It *is* for the good. Continue to be grateful.

The Bible uses multiple metaphors for this process of separating. We call this separation "death." God separates Israel from the nations, the elect from everyone else, the righteous from the sinners, the pure-hearted from the hypocritical. He separates the Holy from the mundane. He separates wheat from chaff. And He smelts the pure from the dross.

Death Is a Refining Process

Looking for a moment into smelting is worthwhile. Smelting is done to mixed metal, such as iron ore that has different metals inside it. Each element in the metal has its own characteristics, just as we humans do. The smelter heats the mixed metal until the different characteristics separate from each other and like unites with like. Most metal is hard. The Bible talks about our hearts as hard, too. Pharoah's heart is perhaps the most obvious example. Pharaoh had a hard heart. No matter how many times God told him that the Israelites were *His* people, Pharoah kept holding power over 'his' people. Then, amidst great heat and friction between two elements of different character—in Moses, God; in Pharoah, ego—God ripped the Israelites from Pharoah's hand through overwhelming power. Pharoah's identity as a god was shattered, and the vehicle for that ego was drowned.

Pharoah's total death was needed for the people of God to separate from Egypt and pop into the limelight on the world stage in the West. If we get the symbolism in the story, it needs only to be the ego that is shattered. The mission of the character of the new people that emerged into freedom is to be light for everyone else—from death, light. The hardness in us needs smelting and separation.

That smelting story is found in Exodus 1-15:21. The Bible also gives a more subtle look at smelting. There was a lampstand in its description of the items to be put in "the holy place" of God's desert tent that traveled with the Israelites to the promised home. The curtains of God's private part of that tent closed off the light coming from the outside world; the only thing lighting God's suite was this one lampstand. To move through Death mode is to journey from a rigid heart closed to God's will and light to having a heart that becomes this lampstand that lights up dark places.

Being God's lampstand. Being a lampstand for God's light involves special characteristics. The first is the strength of unity: the lampstand with all seven arms was made out of one piece of metal. For us, the unity is oneself, one's team(s), and the organization as a team of teams with God. It is in unity of policy, process, people, and purpose. There are no weak links of disunity between God's desire and ours. Patrick Lencioni points out that the most common problem in executive teams is senior leaders seeing themselves as the top dog of their downline. They defend their unit's interests rather than seeing themselves primarily as a member of an executive team that works together, unified under the CEO for the sake of organizational outcomes.[49] He is pointing out mixed-metal executive teams. They struggle, they stress, and they do not shine brightly the pure light of God to effectively and efficiently lead the organization to its land of milk and honey. A good executive team is united. Unity is strength and generates forward movement towards a promised intent.

The second characteristic of our unified lampstand is purity. It was not simply one unified piece of metal; it was 75 pounds of pure gold.[50] It became *pure* gold by the same process God used with Pharoah: smelting. God applies tremendous heat and pressure until you are gold and the impurities are no longer found in you. Your heart, mind, and actions are purified to stand His light and stay in His presence. Purified, now you can be more finely crafted into a work of art and utility. If you and your people have achieved a level of Godly purity, there is much less likelihood of gaps between God's intent, yours, and the business'.

---

[49]Lencioni, Patrick (2006). *Silos, Politics, and Turf Wars: A leadership fable about destroying the barriers that turn colleagues into competitors*. San Francisco: Jossey-Bass

[50] Exodus 25: 31-40 and 37: 17-24

The third characteristic: teachability. Imagine being that 75-pound chunk of metal and being hammered into a beautiful, intricate lampstand. It would take many hammer blows. Sometimes heavy hammering, sometimes incessant delicate taps that reshape you. All in all, lots of getting hammered, the Godly way, being formed to reflect His light in the specific way that 24 karat gold does. Even the oil used for the wicks is not just pure olive oil, but pure olive oil made from "beaten olives."[51] Other translations also have "crushed," "pressed," or "pounded."

The old part of you won't like this; really, it won't. The mind's thoughts will say bad things; the emotions will rage. But the part of you who loves God will rejoice through it or at least be grateful. Remember, God is loving you. He cares about daily decisions on projects to sunset, people to hire, vendors to use, companies to buy, policies to change, how you word that email, all of it because all of it goes into purifying you and adding value to others. Those poundings are vehicles for the power of your love and, hence, for His to increase in your life and the organization. God and the God-filled you lead together for His purposes. Dead people *lead* the way without getting *in* the way.

How to Die, an Example

Though it could just as easily be choosing investors, succession planning, or so many other decisions, let's take delegating as an example of an opportunity to do some dying. Here's how to approach delegating in Death: get intimate enough with God to quickly know if He sees delegating a

---

[51]Exodus 27:20

specific task to a specific person at a specific time negatively, neutrally, or positively.

1. <u>Negative with God: The *No* Zone.</u> Delegating that thing to that person at that time would displease God. Putting a pedophile in charge of training young athletes would be a negative with God. God doesn't want you doing this. Inside you, you know it is wrong. If your choice falls in this first zone, immediately do not do it.
2. <u>Neutral with God: The *Sifting* Zone.</u> While delegating this thing to this person at this time does not go against what God wants, neither did He communicate an active desire for you to do it. The delegation may be *okay* with Him. This zone requires practiced discernment. Sometimes, He is fine with whatever you are about to choose. He gifted you with capabilities, after all, use them. And yet, He may have a preference for whom or when to place, and by His silence, He may invite you to improve your discernment. So, maybe do it your way, maybe don't. Do your spiritual due diligence. First, be rigorously honest about your motivations. If needed, try prayer, wisdom, scripture, and mentors. Or just do it, find out where your decision took your company and your relationship with God, then smile or course-correct.
3. <u>Positive with God: The *Yes* Zone.</u> God moves you to or tells you to delegate this thing to a person or team at such and such a time. If you know it's from Him, even if it is not the logical choice, do it. If you aren't sure, use discernment tools. Run to make Him happy, humbly following instructions right away or at the

appointed time. If others suggest that your delegating is malfeasance, and you realize that you actually decided from a selfish motive rather than because God wanted it, repent, thank your detractors, and fix the problem. But if you truly see it as His will, stay the course.

Recap of dying. 1) Want God more than you want what He does for you. 2) Discern God's will. 3) Live it out: make God's business your business. 4) As much as possible while you yet live, stay dead. Death is the worthiest of challenges. To illustrate the process and to encourage you, here are four examples of CEOs moving through Death mode.

John's Story

John R. Maxwell's is a story of two banks. The first bank John headed reflected who he was in the first six modes; the second bank, who he became in the last four. The first bank carried the name of US President James Monroe. A President metaphor fit John well in those years; he wanted to preside. The second bank, John Marshall Bank, carried the name of a Supreme Court Justice. During his CEO tenure at John Marshall, John aligned himself with justice as conveyed by the Supreme.

Starting out, John paid his dues at a small-town Colorado bank: janitor, teller, and manager. Then he moved to Arlington, VA, the big city out East. There, he mentored under a hard-driving bank president who focused on his own success. During their first lunch, the president told John that they would never be friends. Friendly John asked why. So that the president wouldn't feel bad when he fired him, the president replied. "Well, that's the big city," John told himself. It wasn't warm fuzzy, but he was young. What did he know? To succeed, he dropped into the president's intent and downloaded his wisdom. John was off and running on a path not his own.

After eight years of absorbing the wisdom of the bank president in Arlington, it was time for John to grab the brass ring himself. John gathered investors, raised capital, and assembled a team to open and preside over his own bank, James Monroe Bank.

Outwardly, John's approach was nice-friendly. But, staying in the first six modes of pursuing personal success split him into two people. 1st John was the clean-cut kid from small-town Colorado with a caring "it's about people" style. He attended church on Sundays, played piano for the choir, taught Sunday school, and became a deacon. 2nd John focused on succeeding. If that meant double-martini deal-making and shaving his words to win out over the other guy, well, "that's what you want; it's impersonal, it's cold." It's business. 1st and 2nd John lived together in the same body and had competing values.

Unsurprisingly, something nagged at 1st John. He knew something not quite right about the big city banker that 2nd John was being. He puts it this way:

> I believed that I was on borrowed time, that [despite] all the good things that would happen to me, someday God was going to drop the other shoe and take them away because I wasn't faithful, I wasn't walking with Him, I wasn't living my faith.

John's wife definitely was living her faith, so "it put a lot of tension between my wife and I." Collateral damage. Still, success is, well, being successful; that's what is good, so what is a person to do?

Then, God drew John into wholeness.

The weekend. After years of living in this tension, John attended a men's weekend. John showed up wearing his friendly CEO self-image as armor, but others cared about what was under the image; they cared about *him*. They showed genuine love. The weekend organizers had already knocked and entered the door, submitting their lives to God. They prayed. Businessmen revealed inner secrets and pains, and hugged each other in brotherly affection.

This was definitely outside of John's comfort zone. Except for his son, John had never let *any* adult male hug him. But love melted his armor, and John broke. He surrendered himself to Jesus, God the Redeemer, the Reconciler, the Renewer. Gone was hiding 1st John from 2nd, and 2nd John from 1st. Gone was hiding his normal human vulnerabilities from his wife, his friends, and himself. Gone was hiding from God, and gone was enduring the tension of a divided self.

One John. When John walked through the door and let a wave overtake him, his life changed. Not overnight, but it changed. He came to see his role as President/CEO very differently. Internal and external transition organically happened together, and he transitioned out of James Monroe to lead a bank with only one branch, 12 employees, and $50M. It wasn't about money; it was about God in action. As he focused on God and let God transform him, his intent changed from being about his success to helping a bank renew and grow itself. He was there to do it justice.

He gave the bank a new name, John Marshall Bank, and worked in a new way. He submitted his leadership decisions to God and to His supreme justice. In John's words:

> Before it was 'I want as much as I can get.' And if you weren't giving it to me then something's wrong

here and I'm going to quietly be angry about it and let it build to the point where we're just going to sell this bank. After that it became, I'm going to do what I believe is right. What God has told me is right and fair and is what I'm going to do. So I would pray about that. "What do You see for me?"

Already wealthy in the material sense, his *life* became richer and more meaningful. Accepting his own weakness, he could now utilize God's strength to bring more value to more people. After a dozen years of John and God together leading the John Marshall Bank, it had eight locations, 140 employees, and $1.6B. This happened as a natural consequence of going submitting self and business to God. Take, for instance, the bonus.

The bonus. Like other CEO compensation, John's was much more bonus than salary. Employees received bonuses, too, if they hit the target. At John Marshall, performance was so consistent that some employees planned around their bonuses.

One year, despite everyone's diligence, the bank had a particularly outsized loan failure. The large charge-off dropped the numbers below the set bonus level. But instead of denying them their bonuses, he convinced the board to create a bonus pool, then quietly obliterated 90% of his own bonus and put it in the pool to make everyone else whole. It wasn't an ideological move; he stood before God, knowing that the people God gave him to care for did nothing wrong. *They* hadn't approved the bad loan, and God wouldn't want them to suffer needlessly. Allowing Death to be his mode for a bit, John let his bonus die. But God and John became more one, making John's life much richer.

Wisdom of the heart is one of the things that grew in John. "Everything I do now I look [at] from the perspective of God in my life... I've always believed in God and Jesus Christ; I [just] didn't understand what that meant." Money is God's servant. We are God's servant. When God's business becomes our business, ours is His. We can bank on it.

Death. Peace. Life. Freedom. Fullness. More.

Todd's Story

Todd Bramblett started his third company in 2003. LeverPoint was a global software services consulting firm. He started it with a senior executive who was a longtime friend. It expanded rapidly from two people to three, then five, seven, eight, and twelve. Through the worst of the Great Recession, it still grew. When the economy started gaining its footing at the end of 2009, God rolled LeverPoint a gigantic Wave. Todd was CEO, serial entrepreneur, and God-lover.

Todd surfed well; LeverPoint exploded from a dozen to a team of 125, with revenues increasing commensurately. Todd balanced his smarts and sunburst energy with God's wisdom and his own, which he had gained from experience. He also paid attention to Covey's Seven Habits. Long ago, having walked through the door, Todd knew that the growth he experienced was God's doing. Day by day, he and his 125 rode the wave as it built momentum. More customers, more ROI.

He entered talks to acquire a specialty software consulting firm. That company, small but with access to a stash of cash, turned the tables and offered to acquire LeverPoint. But LeverPoint wasn't yet at the market cap that Todd believed it would soon be, and he wanted to hold on. He had enough business experience to know that LeverPoint was poised to give him the ability to retire young, very young, and in style, if he just held on for another year or two. If he sold now, he'd have to keep working, especially since the offer was 20% cash and 80% stock. Todd knew his company, the market, and the wisdom of waiting: only four years later, the company had a staff of 625.

Todd also had enough experience walking with God to know that the choice of whether to hold or sell wasn't up to him. LeverPoint, like all else that belonged to Todd, belonged to God. Anyone who walks through the door knows that, but it's in Death that the pressure of living up to what you know presses on you with full force. You can see what's at play in Todd's decision: years of more work or a life of freedom. And employees have opinions. And the family has opinions. And investors have opinions. And you live with the repercussions. Todd hiked into the woods and prayed so that he could distance himself from distractions and focus on God. He knew that God was not only Lord of the universe but his best friend, so he talked openly. "Lord," he said, "this thing is hitting it. We're going to skyrocket; I can feel it. I don't want to sell. I don't want to sell."

Of course, God is God. So when God speaks, EF Hutton listens. Or, anyway, *should* listen. Todd reports: "And He said, clear as day, 'Sell. It will be good.'" But Todd already knew what was good: hold the company, sell later. Cognitive dissonance rang in Todd's ears.

What to do?

Since we don't know what we don't know, and since we cannot know what it is that we don't know that we don't know, the unsurrendered life goes with what it knows and leaves the rest to worry about itself. In the surrendered life, it's not that easy. Part of what the surrendered person knows is that God knows *everything,* and we do not. So if God says something, even if it goes against what we know, the surrendered life listens. How did the Israelites put it at Mount Sinai? "All that the Lord has spoken we will do."[52]

But 3,400 years later, when you're alone as God's word falls in a forest, it's easy to say the word didn't fall and dismiss what you heard as unreal. How easy to think: 'Wait, was that really God? It makes no sense; God wouldn't say "sell," and God loves me. I should ask again later. I must not be hearing clearly.' How easy it is to keep ourselves from being dead. I'll die tomorrow (maybe), not today. If that really was God, surely, He'll tell me again and then, I'll be sure. It's better that today I hold on to the company.

The mode of Death is predicated on enough of you being in love with God to surrender the next most difficult thing to surrender. "And I'm like, 'oh my gosh'," says Todd. "It seems that wisdom in the face of this things says I should not sell right now. But He's saying, 'sell.' Okay, I'm going to do it; I'm going to sell. And I did." Even if he didn't call it that, Todd knew he was supposed to be in Death mode. His soul pulled out its sword, determined to fight to the death.

Todd did what God said, choosing what felt like personal death, honoring God's wave, and walking in the truth bigger than self. With 80% of the payment being stock, God kept using that decision as a way to massage the edge of Todd's faith and keep him going deeper into Death, day after day, year after year, as stock value fluctuated. In the end, God blessed Todd in the regular way of financial abundance,

---

[52] Exodus 19:8 (MEV).

too. But even if the new owners had blown it and the stock tanked. Whatever.

Death. Peace. Life. Freedom. Fullness. More.

Wayland's Story

Up until he caught the big wave, Wayland Coker was a Lieutenant Commander in the US Navy. Watching the wave come at him, he took a risk to surf it. He resigned his commission and went private. Soon, he was organizing teams of people, including 3-Star Generals who recently outranked him.

Wayland implemented a new type of war game for the joint and coalition forces. Each war game took years of behind-the-scenes prep, and his staff grew. It was a high-pressure transformative contribution to the nation's military preparedness, to his team of 50 and their families, and to his own bottom line. He lived in Harvest. Then the Great Recession hit, and he went from Harvest to famine. He lost the contract, lost close to 75% of his workforce, and lost his lifestyle.

Wayland did what CEOs who work with God do when the bottom drops out. He asked himself if his relationship with God had been on track or if he had been fooling himself. He took an honest look. His words echo those you've probably heard before if maybe the particulars were different:

> I had an 11,000 square foot house on 8 acres, I had an airplane, I had a yacht, I had a Harley, I had a Porsche, I had seven cars… and we still paid our tithes and were faithful to church. I gave lots of

money away. I had a charitable organization. I gave to orphanages and sports programs. I thought I was doing [right]. You know, isn't this what you do when you use your resources but you enjoy it too? But I'm thinking, 'Lord, am I not doing enough for your kingdom? Am I enjoying this a bit too much?'

"Isn't this what you do?" Ride God's wave, contribute your talents, harvest the benefits, enjoy the good things, and share from your abundance: isn't this what you do? Yes, it is. Death just reminds us that we didn't Wave ourselves up and that we don't own the Harvest. We own nothing. God gives us everything. Always. Every moment. Including our lives. We serve at the pleasure of the Chief, not the other way around.

To good purpose, everything in this world has a shelf life. God provides things that sustain us but also stamps an expiry date on every created item. How else would we remember that the Almighty sustains us than by providing food we enjoy *for a while*? If food never spoiled, we would never remember the One from whom all food comes. Spoilage is necessary. Seeing how long it takes us to get over spoilage of the things in our life is how we see who we put in charge of refrigeration: God or our created identity, the Almighty's will, or our self-effort. No matter how hard we work, how smart we are, how courageous, and even how obedient we are to what we think God wants, in the end, identity fails us. That's okay; God remains with us. *Who loves you, baby?*

God has a way of smelting the lives of those who want Him, surfacing self-oriented desires to be burnt off. The smelting fire burns especially hot in Death mode. In Death, you allow the incineration of your identity's control over decision-making. In Death, God strengthens your obedience ability. And your organization's ability to operate in the first six modes—not just with God but *under God*—expands with you.

In Wayland's case, God kept reminding him of the story of Joseph. In Genesis 37-50, we see Joseph go from being a servant of one of Pharoah's top officials to spending years in Pharoah's prison. There, Joseph died to his dreams. Once that happened, *voila,* he became CEO under God and operated as CEO in Pharoah's palace. God reassured Wayland that it would be challenging, but He would still be there for him. We'll see the rest of Wayland's story in CEO mode.

The real question in Death is this: Is there something you hold on to more strongly than you hold onto God?

Ted's Story

Meet Ted Davies, former Chairman & CEO of the $100M Altamira Technologies Corporation, and you meet someone alive and in motion. He attends to business with love and brings value to his 400+ employees, their families, and other stakeholders. You wouldn't guess that behind his smile and success, Ted Davies had endured death.

Ted married his college sweetheart, bought a house in the suburbs, and made his way up the ladder in government contracting. They raised two wonderful children and took the dog for walks. He made partner at the renowned Booz Allen Hamilton consulting firm. His future was set to be something akin to Jimmy Stewart's in It's a Wonderful Life. By his own admission, he had a blessed life. "I was rockin' and rollin'," Ted said. "Life was great... for about 40 years." His attitude and ability stacked family and career successes one on top of each other. Then God moved Ted to *more*.

My wife wanted me to [leave] Booz Allen. I went to church and prayed one day. I had tons of late nights, and you could tell that it was wrecking our marriage. And you could tell that something had to give...

God let me know in my heart, "I've given you this family. This family is a gift to you from Me, and a career is just a career." I resigned on the spot.

There was that voice in my heart. He gave me my family for a reason, and I'm going to voluntarily walk away [from them] because I like the job I'm in? Because I'm comfortable? When you're in [the decision], oh my God, it destroys you. But when I step back later and look at it, it was like, why would there even be a decision?... It's a good example of trusting God. I had *no* idea what I was going to do next; I was scared out of my mind. [But] I've never regretted [leaving the job] a day in my life, and I would have made a lot more money where I was.

Then God rolled Ted another wave that would move him farther still. A year after Ted left Booz Allen, his wife got Lupus. For four brutal years, they went through ups and downs, hospitals, and finally, her death. But Ted sees God and, therefore, sees good.

I almost cry when I think about it—if I would have left them [for career], what would she and those kids have gone through? I couldn't have lived with myself, and God knew. God knew what the plan was going to be.

That was a fundamental turning point in a partnership with God. If I would have made a different decision, I know it wouldn't have been anywhere near as spiritual, the journey that I'm on right now. And being able to sit in that [CEO's] chair and take bad news and still handle it and still discern what God wants me to do with that. If you don't have that partner [in God], where do you turn when things don't go well?

Death. Peace. Life. Freedom. Fullness. More.

Chapter Eleven

CEO

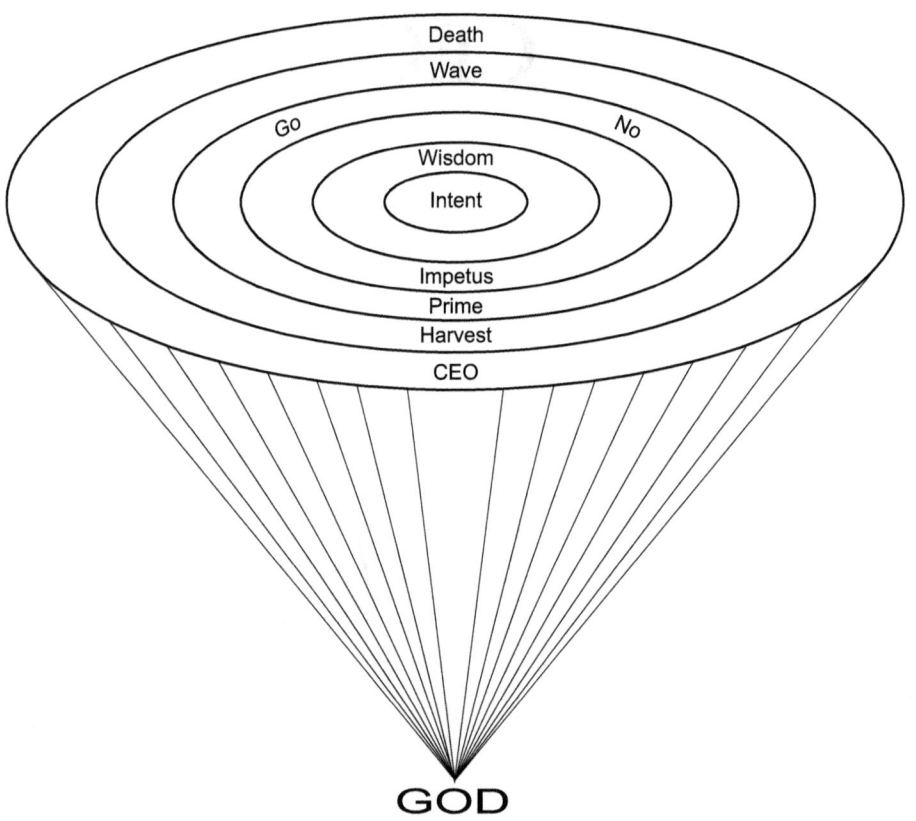

Now it was after the death of Moses, the Lord's servant, that the Lord said to Joshua son of Nune, Moses' page, saying: "Moses my servant died. So now, rise and cross this Jordan, you and this whole people, to the land that I Am gives to them, to the children of Israel."

Joshua 1:1-2
Author's translation

You wake up to find yourself dead. Your life has been jiggered. Something is missing. Aha! *You* are somewhat missing, the old you, that is. And yet you are also full. God fills you. And here you are, still a leader. Now what?

Resurrection. Living the new you. The new streamlined, simplified, dethroned, un-obnoxious, lightened up, differently empowered, dangerously effective you.

It's not so dramatic, really. We have not died bodily. For our identity, though, it is exactly such a moment. In the first six modes, we retained control. In so doing, we limited our organizations to the extent of our vision and ability, felt the burden was ultimately ours, and felt that success was ours to claim and failure ours to suffer. Not knowing it, we lived in a dim cave wrapped in the cloth of control. As more than one former CEO has said, "I'd never do that again!"

Becoming aware of God's call, we walked on through the Door and let the light of God guide us. We dove into Death, day by day, decision by decision, action by action, giving way to His control, letting the Spirit of God blow a hole through us until one day we notice that we are His flute. His Spirit inside and around us, He took us out of the cave that had kept us. Now, in God, with God, we see anew, walk anew, talk anew. We gave control to God, and He gave us new clothes.

Wayland's Coda

When I checked in with Wayland a year after he told me of his loss in Death mode, he still hadn't gotten back his big Navy contract. But, he reported, large contracts had come at him unexpectedly from a new source.

Through Death, Wayland had been humbled and rearranged. He had put God back at the top of the food chain. This time, in a way more real, thorough, and deep, Wayland gave God all rights to guide his life in Intent. From here on out it would be God's will, not Wayland's. Once Wayland got the relationship straight, Jesus wasn't going to waste Wayland's talent.

At the start of COVID-19, Wayland posted a note on LinkedIn to see if anyone needed a high-level logistics person. At the time, the US government was scrambling to get vaccines and medical devices to the public. Just at that moment, the team of PhDs and MDs in charge of making it happen realized they needed a business and logistics person. A few days after he posted his CV, he was contacted. Health and Human Services assigned him a place where he could be influential in helping organize their effort. He brought in industry experts, cleared red tape, prevented them from hitting logistics potholes, and arranged a thousand and one logistics details. The rest is history: life-saving medical equipment and millions of vaccines distributed quickly, saving so many lives. Wayland didn't do that alone, but he was a key person placed, as only God can do, in the right spot at the right time, with the right knowledge and skills.

To facilitate this logistical feat, God worked with Wayland and Wayland with God simultaneously in all ten modes: Intent, Wisdom, Impetus, *Go,* No, Prime, Wave, Harvest, Death, and CEO. Wayland benefited from financial harvest and something much greater: soul harvest. Whereas his story began with him helping the Navy be more efficient at killing people as part of national defense, now he engaged in a different kind of national defense: he helped prevent possibly hundreds of thousands or perhaps millions of people from suffering and death. The richness this brings one's soul is inestimable. And because he had made it through Death mode, he didn't have the stress that comes with depending on the position for one's peace—he knew that *I-Will-Be* arranged it and was with him to make it happen. This time, he was not a CEO in title; he was now CEO in God's world. Humbly walking in reasonable risk by having faith at work is being the Chief's Executive Officer.

Naturally, before the complete unification of your will with God's will, *yours* will pop up now and again. You'll have it your way, on your own, without God. That's okay. Cry, repent, laugh, move on. You keep getting closer with God. Separation between you and God becomes more and more subtle. But once you, like Jacob, finish wrestling through the night and a new dawn breaks and God gives you a new name,[53] don't give credence to thoughts and feelings of fear or lack. Newly named and newly clothed, occupy your new home. Especially as God brings new challenges.

New Things

God tells us. "Forget the former things; do not dwell on the past. See, I am doing a new thing! Now it springs up; do you not perceive it? I am making a way in the wilderness and streams in the wasteland."[54]

The apostle Paul declares: "We were buried with Him by baptism into death, that just as Christ was raised up from the dead by the glory of the Father, even so we also should walk in newness of life."[55]

What will you say to your executive team? To the investors and customers and the homeless person on the sidewalk at the entrance to your building? You can no longer judge

---

[53] See Genesis 32:21-31
[54] Isaiah 43:18-19 NIV
[55] Romans 6:4 MEV

as you formerly did. What you think is bad may not be bad; what you think is good may not be good. Jesus said, "Do not judge."[56] And while dead people are better at discerning than those who are out for the success of their identity, dead people don't *judge*; not others, not themselves. They leave that to God. So now what? What *do* dead people do?

Whatever they do, *you* don't. You do nothing on your own without Him. Your identity doesn't make decisions and take action; you and God do. Dead people have more room inside them for Him to live. The God who created the nature that abhors a vacuum won't leave you empty. He fills you, He lives in you; with God in your nerves and veins, mind and heart, it is not exactly *you* doing things, nor is it God alone since you are still there. A more peaceful, hopeful, and probably more enjoyable you.

It's His business now. You are a different CEO; you are the Chief's Executive Officer. You execute *His* intent. Sometimes, you need to be His secretary of state, sometimes press secretary, sometimes secretary of the treasury, and sometimes the Chief Engagement Officer. And all that is simply His Administrative Assistant. In whatever your role-de-jour, you 'do the do' to execute the Chief's will. *That* is working with God. In your person, you incorporate all nine previous modes, easily accessing each and flowing through them as necessary for any given situation.

> *In whatever your role-de-jour, you 'do the do' to execute the Chief's will. That is working with God.*

---

[56]Matthew 7:1 (NASB)

Still not falling prey to self, you release your harvest of money and time as God directs; your jailer is dead, and he left you the keys. You speak with discernment to each stakeholder. Yes, nothing less than speaking for God and acting on His behalf as best you can. You join a most worthy club.

WALK SILENT, WALK DEEP

Now, we slow down. No more rushing. Time moves on, and we are in sync with it. Every surrendered moment is time used to the fullest. You get so much done and yet remain present, at peace, and full of life. Filled with the eternal, here we are, in time but not of it. New situations are in each moment. What are the two most important words of advice in this book? Stay dead.

Keep going until there is nothing left of your will that is separate from God's will. It's doubtful that the first time you enter the mode of Death, the Lord will keep you there without respite until you are completely and totally dead. Many say, "I surrender my life to You;" few indeed do it so thoroughly that they never take back any part of it. "But He gives more grace," as Jesus' brother James said,[57] and gives us breaks from daily dying. Sometimes, things are actually easy.

Stay dead but stay alert, for the battle continues.

If you garden, you know that when you start pulling up a weed, its root sometimes snaps in self-protection to ensure the weed's regrowth. It leaves some of itself unnoticed underground, feeding on the soil and regrowing. Then, in the spring, up it springs. It is the same with the weed of self.

---

[57] James 4:6 (ESV)

We pull up the weed that we see and think we are done. We think, "*I'm good. I'm submitted to God.*" Maybe we don't need to die right now on this thing.

On the other hand, maybe "I'm good" was not *God's* thought; it may have been the root of self-identity regrowing. Do you love God enough to please Him this time, too? CEOs are asked to dig deeper and pull up more self-root, day by day by day.

The battle continues. Our decision to die directs us down the path of living with God wherever we are, including the workplace. This demands being awake. You know the forces at work trying to trip you. And they usually do it with a smile. James continues his "But He gives more grace" statement: "Therefore, it says, 'God opposes the proud but gives grace to the humble.'"[58] Pride glazes our glasses, blurs our vision, and warps our walk in a thousand tiny moments. The battle is to stay humble. Amidst joy, peace, and bounty, battle the will of self that comes to cage you and separate you from your Beloved.

Without vigilance, it is easy to find yourself on autopilot, missing a desire's source. It's a slow, subtle slope to self. Return to the first chapter and discern the three sources: your will, His will, and all other sources. Ask God for His help, ask yourself your motivation, be honest, and act courageously.

At the end of his 40-year tenure as CEO of People Israel, Inc., Moses addressed the company with a farewell speech. He said:

> The Lord your God is bringing you into a good land,
> a land of brooks of water, of fountains and springs,

---

[58]This is a foundational Biblical principal. For instance, Proverbs 3:34, composed 700-1000 years before James, contains the same statement.

flowing forth in valleys and hills... a land where you will eat food without scarcity, in which you will not lack anything...

Beware that you do not forget the Lord your God by not keeping His commandments... otherwise, when you have eaten and are satisfied, and have built good houses and lived in them, and when your herds and your flocks multiply, and your silver and gold multiply, and all that you have multiplies, then your heart will become proud and you will forget the Lord your God who brought you out from the land of Egypt, out of the house of slavery.

Otherwise, you may say in your heart, 'My power and the strength of my hand made me this wealth.' But you shall remember the Lord your God, for it is He who is giving you power to make wealth, that He may confirm His covenant.[59]

Do not for a moment think: "*I built it.*" If you forget and think you got this or that project done, be careful. A dead person does not build anything. It was probably some imagined identity of yours that built it. But then fear not: repent, course-correct, laugh, and move on with and under God Almighty.

Implementation Question

What structure, process, person, or value do you need to add or remove from your life, project, team, or organization so that the Holy Spirit can flow more freely through you and through the situation?

---

[59]Deuteronomy 8:7-18 (NASB)

Clothes Shopping: The CEO's 5W Suit

Enough warnings; onwards! Now that you are dead and God rises through you, you need new clothes. Implementing God's will, the CEO clothes himself or herself in practicalities. Pieces of advice from CEOs can be found in Appendix A; here, we look at the 5 W's.

Why. For God so loved the world.[60] Dead to self, we want to do as God does. If that's what He wants, that's what we want. If that's who He loves, that's who we love. For God so loves the world, therefore we so love the world, that's why. You love God. Now put on your undergarments of Why and go love the world.

When. CEOs are highly aware of time, the worthy opponent. A CEO in Prime uses strategic and tactical efficiencies to best time the organization's varying productive capacities. A CEO in CEO mode will incorporate those into a bigger efficiency: obedience to God Almighty, who sees and guides from beyond time. That, of course, demands trust, but you've been building that. Operating in God's time, you hold your plans loosely, even the ones you prayed about. There you are, present in time and place with I-Will-Be, who you don't control. Wearing your undergarments of Why, now don your hat of When.

Who is What. *What* is the action expression of *Who*. Since love is *who* you are, serving is *what* you do. You serve because it's who you are when God is in you, not because it's what you *should* do. Your feeling of obligation melts into pure desire to express love. If you serve motivated by "should" alone, that would mean one part of you

---
[60]John 3:13-17

is disconnected from another. Your "want" should quickly align with your "should." Think about that for your particular What (that you do). Wearing your undergarments of Why and your hat of When, now put on your shirt of What.

How. Your relationship with God reveals the how. This book is part of that. Having gone through all nine previous modes, it is Immanuel (literally, "With Us is God") with you and you with I-Will-Be. How you do it is between you and Him, contextualized in community. However you do it, you are a vehicle for heaven on earth, doing your best to have yourself and your team align with the will of God. Sometimes, that means using the word "God;" often, it does not.

Prayer in How. The CEO is a two-way street. In CEO, you also bring the needs of your people up to God. You variously advocate, defend, reason, plead, listen, maintain patience, and claim goodness for them. You do what you can within the intimacy of your relationship with God. You are an organizational warrior.

In addition to your organizational skill, prayer—perhaps accompanied by study, fasting, time alone, and/or symbolic actions—can be more consequential than any meeting you have, directive you give, or any consultant you hire. God can do things for your staff behind the scenes that you can't. Advocate for them.

As Abraham advocated to avert the fate of Sodom and Gomorrah, so you bargain boldly and respectfully.[61] As Jacob did not stop wrestling the God-man until he agreed to bless Jacob and his family, you also wrestle through your night that God and man may bless your organizational family.[62]

---

[61]Genesis 18
[62]Genesis 32:24-31

As Moses reasoned and even drew a line in the sand with God to ensure that He would not destroy but accompany the people He gave him,[63] so you stand for your people. Do you love? Then advocate. And as Jesus dedicated his impending physical death to the unification of his people with his Father "that they may have my joy fulfilled in themselves,"[64] in prayer you multiply or even transfer blessing that is or could have been yours to your people. That's how to be CEO. Wearing your undergarments of Why, your hat of When, and your shirt of What, now put on your pants of How.

Where. Anyplace, and the entire world. Since the world is a big place, or at least it used to be, *where* in the world? You'll know. At any given moment, the right place may be:

- where you are,
- where you want to be, or
- where you should be.

Where you are. The right place may be exactly where you are, in the organization you are in, in the role you are in, with the people you are with. If God is in your office, it's the best place in the world.

Where you want to be. Maybe God moved on, but you are still where He used to be. You will know if God beckons you elsewhere. As the Lord said, "My sheep hear my voice, I know them, and they follow me."[65] Is desire stirring in your heart for elsewhere?

---

[63]Exodus 32:7-14
[64]John 17:13 (ESV)
[65]John 10:27 (CSB)

Where you should be. And maybe the right place to be is neither where you are nor where you desire to be. Maybe God prepared a home for you someplace where you simply *know* you should be. One day, after four months of being in limbo, the voice of God dropped in and said to me: "**Newark.**" I knew He meant I should move to Newark, NJ. But within a fraction of a second, the hope and question mark of Newark, DE (which, to me, was a nicer place) popped into my mind. A fraction of a second after that, He followed "**Newark**" by repeating "**Newark**" and adding, "**New Jersey.**" That was that. Not where I was, not where I wanted to be, but where I should be. Projects, career moves, strategic plans, vendors, events, property, and personnel choices all have a specific place in God's world.

Because God was there, Newark became my home, the best place in the world. I loved Newark! I did my best to live out life as one of the Chief's executive officers there, making whatever contribution I made to the place's physical, financial, emotional, mental, social, and spiritual well-being. Those years were rich. God-things happen when a CEO lives awake at the intersection of is, want, and should. Wearing your undergarments of Why, your hat of When, your shirt of What, and your pants of How, now put on your shoes of Where and walk there.

Fully clothed in new clothes, walk until it is time to stop. Do not stop too early or too late. You will know when it is time.

Complete Success is Succession. God's business continues beyond you. None of your business now; He carries His organization from leader to leader. Though you have for years groomed someone(s) for your transition or done your due diligence in finding someone, you do not release your organization to the next CEO. Rather, you now fully release it into God's hands.

God arranges succession, and, as always, you discern and align with His plans as best you can and let go. If the organization succeeds better than when you were with it, it's a credit to the foundation God set through you. If the organization fails, it may be because you haven't been working to replace yourself with systems, structure, and people. If so, ask for forgiveness and God's help being less self-centered, and move on. Or maybe you did fine, but the organization needed to fail for some celestial reason you can't see. In any case, with gratitude, release your organization into the Sea of Forgetfulness and stay with God. On the one hand, there is a big change, but on the other, there is none.

As Jesus departed, he invested his disciples as CEOs, each with his own mission, then succinctly said: "Behold, I am with you always, to the end of the age."[66] In God's succession plan for People Israel, Inc., Moses had spent decades mentoring Joshua. But Moses symbolically climbed a mountain toward God and accepted his death, as God gave the helm to Joshua. Moses did not need to be concerned, nor do you, for as the Lord told Joshua:

> As I was with Moses, so I will be with you. I will not let go of you and I will not leave you. Be strong and courageous, for you will lead this people to inherit the land... Just be strong and very courageous.[67]

---

[66] Matthew 28:20 (ESV)
[67] Joshua 1:5-7 (author's translation)

Endinning (Ending, Beginning, End of Inning)

The end is as the beginning, just different. Do you *Go*? Do you *No*? You know. If you are not sure, ask Him. Do you love? Of course, love with wisdom. I-Will-Be is always with you.

This is your commission: make life good for your people while you still have them. Leverage all your skills for better outcomes, just as you always have. But now with peace, joy, and strength in the midst of even the most difficult situations, continuing to be that lampstand for His light. The government is on His shoulders.[68] He arranges, He supplies, He judges, and He communicates. Stay yoked with Him, listen and obey, and where there is silence, find out why or, at some point, tell God what you are going to do, ask Him to be with you, then do it and keep listening. Prepare your next-gen Josh or your 12 disciples so that God's baby (what you used to call your organization) can keep growing without you.

The modes are your shepherd's staff for you to lean on, and to wave to guide your staff of employees. They are an operating model for organizational effectiveness and efficiency. The modes help you balance competing organizational values in practice. The modes even guide your team and interpersonal relations. And awareness of modality attunes you to the movement of God so you and the business can stay in time with Him. This is deep agility. Teach the ten modes to others to keep yourselves aware, accountable, and close to God.

---

[68] Isaiah 9:6

> *The modes are your shepherd's staff.*

Avoda: Workship. Let your work be your prayer, and your prayer be your work. In Hebrew, "prayer," "work," "worship," and "service" are all the same word: *avoda* (ah-vō-DAH). Make it your business to make His business your business, that it may be His business here on earth. You will be His warrior and witness. And you and yours will be taken along for the beauty, wonder, strength, glory, and Life of Him who created you. And it will be well. And one day, one day, the glory of God will be revealed.[69]

Don't wait to deepen your relationship with God. Don't wait to be more genuinely humble.

Don't wait to free yourself from what people who are not intimate with God defined for you as "good."

Don't wait to give up all the results of your work to Him each day.

Don't wait to give up your goals and desires the moment you see that you are holding them more closely than God.

Don't wait to give up that position, that promotion, that IPO, or the rooted belief that you deserve what you want for yourself. Give them to God; if He returns them to you, it will be a far more precious gift, and, it won't own you. Trust that what you empty, He will fill if needed.

Don't wait to jump on the surfboard of God's waves to realize the abundance of God's harvest. And don't wait to give up that wonderful harvest with a *"Thank you, my Lord!"* and start again in trust and love from a new shore.

---

[69] Isaiah 40:1-5

That is freedom and safety all in one. It all came from God. Again and again, return it all to Him. Do whatever it takes to stay with Him because it is He who is the treasure, not the things He brings. Those are delightful but second prize. In your soul, own nothing. Don't wait to give God the joy of your desire for Him.

Be strong and very courageous, and remember that He is always with you.

Now and always, work with God.

Appendix A

WHE BUILT IT

Some grace-filled stories were not included in the main text. To add richness, here are direct quotes from double CEOs—Chief Executive Officer and Chief's Executive Officer.

Ted Davies on 'Who built it?'

I would say it's a combination of a bunch of great people. I wouldn't sit here and say God built this company. I think God builds people and the people build companies.

John R. Maxwell on 'Who built it?'

Who built the banks? God. Plain and simple. Me—God through me—I was His vessel here on earth that completed the work that He wanted to complete.

Jim Hadley on humility

Everybody wants to be the CEO and have the title and have a thousand employees or more and have $100M revenue. But I think if you put people in those positions and live that for one day, they're like: 'I don't want this, this is crazy, this is insane.' ... I want to be a great husband, a great follower of Christ, a great father. I will let God be the governor of what this [company] is going to be because I know that if it got too big, I could self-destruct.

Steve Casbon[68] on finding investors and on talent development

<u>On finding investors</u>: So many times, has this happened, in every one of our deals, where I've strived, I've called on

---

[68] Managing Partner, Ambassador Development Group

people, I've made appointments, I've called them back, I email them back, I do the follow up... and then I feel like I'm just wearing people out. And then I just give up. And somehow God moves in just the right person at the right time. And it encourages me or gives me a sign to show me that He's in it. Or one of my advisors will bring in a couple of new investors. But it almost seems that those moments when I just kind of give up, and truly all I do is I pray: "God I can't do this." And God says, "Okay, now I have you where I need you because when this works, you got nowhere to point but up."

<u>On talent development</u>: We use the Culture Index. It assesses really how God wired us. It's our desire to get every teammate in alignment with the gifting that God gave them... and then get you in a position with either our company or maybe somewhere else in alignment with who you were wired to be... I believe God has a purpose and has designed everybody with a plan and a purpose... But does everybody have to subscribe to that? No, absolutely not. And even the leaders in our companies don't have to describe it that way. But that's why we do it, and we believe the Culture Index is a way to get people in alignment with who they are.

Mark Whitacre on Leadership and on Purpose

<u>On leadership</u>: Mature believers are all servant leaders... A C-suite executive would approach any business situation—clinical trial, sales, marketing—from servant leadership: in this meeting, "God how can I serve you?"

<u>On purpose</u>: I believe that God puts us in the marketplace to have a sphere of influence around us—five hundred

to a thousand people—key vendors, key customers, employees who report to you... [You influence] more through action than words. Then it opens up an opportunity [to connect them with God]. So I look at the business world a little differently. I feel like it's to reach the lost.

Tom Toth[69] on how God clearly shows up at work, and on whether to talk about God

<u>On how God shows up</u>: It's the people that God brings to you. I mean the folks that I have came out of apparently nowhere. *Apparently.*

<u>On whether to talk about God at work</u>: I figure if we create a good environment, [and] somebody comes [onboard to the team] if they're not a believer, if we have a good environment, a Godly environment... we don't *talk* about God. Now we pray when we're all eating lunch together... so there's clearly a God mode in the breaking of bread at least. It's all about example to me. It's not about me preaching Christ, it's me living as if I love people, which I do.

Todd Bramblett on surfing with God

Peter had control over whether he decided to put his leg over the boat.[70] If you want to walk on water, you gotta make a choice to step. But if you think you can walk on water and you're the genius, you're mistaken. It's a partnership: you step, God holds the water in place. Peter can lift his leg and he can do what he can do, but he can't make [the project] go into orbit without God making the wave happen.

---

[69]Tom Toth Sr., President and CEO, Toth Financial
[70]For accounts of Peter's walk on water, see Matthew 14:22-23 and Mark 6:45-52

Paul Bice[71] on surfing and on being CEO

<u>On surfing</u>, *referring to the story in Genesis 22 where God asks Abraham to sacrifice his son Isaac*... And in my little Bible it says "God will provide." And when I read that, it just lifts off the page. Woah... Okay, I'm going to keep doing this and see what happens... The amount of detail that Father will go through to assure you that He's right there in the midst of it... I've have [seen it happen] over and over again... We serve a God that speaks, that guides, that directs, that is very intimately involved. You know the scripture; "Lord give me eyes to see, ears to hear." That's because He's doing things all around us all the time.

<u>On being CEO</u>: I cannot grip it, I cannot control it, I cannot think of it as mine... Each client relationship I have is not mine to own or mine to manipulate... it's put there. Listen to people, take care of people.

Jeff Skeen on lots of things

<u>On being CEO</u>: I don't [now] feel like I'm a CEO because I want to be a CEO; I feel like He's given me the things I need to be one so therefore I *should be* one. ... I had teammates that had followed me through the trenches. If I wasn't willing to sacrifice, who would? Like I don't believe in my vision, I don't believe in God's vision, right?

<u>On purpose and time</u>: Are you serving *Him*? Are you really making a difference, are you serving those around you for the kingdom, something beyond just being the CEO of a publicly traded company?

---

[71]Regional President & Founding Officer, John Marshall Bank; Regional Executive & Founding Officer, James Monroe Bank

<u>On relating to employees</u>: The world is like: you're my employee, I pay you, you'll do what I say no matter what. I'm like: I'm paying you and I'm privileged to have you on my team, and I can't wait to find out what we can do together… As a CEO I'm there to nurture them. Because if I take care of them, they take care of the company… There's the head of Coca Cola going taking people to clear out debris from [his employees] homes, and that's publicly traded. He's right there with them… From a CEO's perspective you have to love people like Christ did. They have to know that they're not a widget in your kingdom, that they're actually a part of *the* kingdom [of God].

<u>On doing the right thing</u>: We got to a point where the Board is like: 'you have to let go of your business partners' executives so we can make bank covenants… I said, 'I'll get back to you.' Prayed about it; talked to my wife. She was not happy with my decision, but what I decided to do was to give up my income—my salary—until the company got on board, on track.

<u>On risk</u>: They invested with me a lot of money. They have set expectations of return with their money. If I hit that return, high five to Jeff Skeen; if I don't hit that return, good bye to Jeff Skeen. For 26 years, for the most part, my IR was 25% a year, through 2 or 3 recessions. It's God's control.

<u>On career</u>: What I don't know is where God is going to take [my career], but what I do know is He's going to take it somewhere… It is really neat when you change the perspective of what you're doing in your life, in your career [to see God in control of it].

<u>On God</u>: God has a sense of humor.

Appendix B

THE WORKING WITH GOD PRAYER SHEET

Before you start an initiative, pray. Pray not just for the success of the initiative, but that what you want and what He wants may be as one all along the way. Once you have an intent, ready your heart for prayer. Be still of mind and calm of breath. Offer yourself and the landscape of the initiative to God. Be ready to write down insights that He gives you for each mode. Once you recognize that God is present with you and listening, tell the Lord your intent and give it to Him. He may respond to your intent. If you think He might have planted an intent in you, ask Him if it was from Him. Either way, write down His response for future reference. And if He does not command you to end the project or not to undertake the initiative, follow up with these queries. Pause to listen intently for His communication to you and/or inside you after each.

1) **Wisdom:** Lord, please grant me the wisdom to see and hear what is wise. What should I pay attention to as I approach *name of initiative* ?
2) **Impetus:** Lord, do I have sufficient and correct emotional imperative to launch now?
3) **Go:** Lord, what are the things I should do now?
4) **No:** Lord, what should I regulate? What should I avoid?
5) **Prime:** Lord, what else would you show me about the things you have told me?
6) **Door:** Lord, I give all of me to You, including this project. I give you the results of any further efforts in this project. It is Yours to speed, to slow, to stop, to magnify, or to change. To remove me or to keep me in. And if any of these happen, I am still with You as You are with me. I am ready for what comes

next as long as it is Your desire. May it all be for your glory. Amen.

7) **Wave:** Lord, where should this land me and/or the clients?

8) **Harvest:** Lord, I am grateful for the opportunity to __*verb*__ [have / help / learn / land / navigate to / do / say / enter / grow / invest / step-into / provide / take / be / etc.] __*where He said he in #7 that He wants to bring you*__. I own and celebrate this initiative for as long as You wish me to be there. All praise to You whose will is perfect in this and in all things. I love You.

9) **Death:** Lord, what thing, less than holy, should I die to in this?

10) **CEO:** Lord, here I am, ready.

ACKNOWLEDGEMENTS

Each thing is exactly what it is because of everything that came before it. Had they been otherwise, this book would have been different. I give thanks to God for all things that have existed and that now exist, be they pleasurable or unpleasurable.

Skipping the unpleasurable, I must call out some specific people for thanks. This book would not have happened had my parents, literature lovers both, not been who they were. Professor Robert M. Latzer, with his exacting and inquisitive mind, taught me to ask questions, think carefully, and see with eyes of wonder. Julia Wohl Latzer, with her loving care for her students, family, and community members, modeled for me a strong ethical compass, straightforward speech, and practical wisdom. These thanks are grossly insufficient to do their lives justice.

I am most grateful to my radiant wife and partner Shira Leiba Chaya Lotzar, who shares the passion for God and for people at work. She said only good things when I spent so many hours writing instead of doing things for career, house, home, and her.

This book owes the best of its business content to Professor Ichak Adizes, Founder of Adizes Institute Worldwide. His surpassing insight into human behavior and organizational dynamics is broad, and deeply rooted in realpolitik. I am highly grateful to him, and also to Shoham Adizes for his most excellent teaching of the Adizes methodology.

Thank you to Professor Emeritus Ronald Dorr for teaching me the beauty of disciplined writing. My thanks also go to Brad Byrd for guidance in the initial phases of writing and to Dr. Tracey C. Jones of Tremendous Leadership, who had the experience, wisdom, talent, and unflagging positivity that encouraged and shepherded this book to its final format. Anything poor about this book is due to my own lack of clarity and wisdom.

I also owe a debt of gratitude to a great many Bible, religion, theology, and God-teachers. There were the formal teachers at the Solomon Schecter School and the Jewish Theological Seminary of America. There were those at St. John Fisher University and at James Madison College of Michigan State University who taught me how to research, organize, and analyze. Those at the Paul Baerwald School of Social Work at The Hebrew University of Jerusalem taught me how to think like a decision-making administrator who integrates organizational efficiency and empathy for individuals.

There were also numerous friends and compatriots, even momentary associates, who were informal teachers, thought-developers, mentors, goads, inspirers, sparring partners, and messengers of God. To call out a very few influencers: Rabbi Shlomo Carlebach, Werner Erhard, Reverend Dr. Thomas Keinath, J. Thomas Johnson, Marc Palen, and forever friend Frederick Vincent Burckbuchler, Jr. There were the powerful authors of long ago whose thought influenced this book, authors who were lovers of truth and lovers of God.

Moreover, this book and I owe an insurmountable debt of gratitude to my premier teacher-mentor, far and away the greatest Chief's Executive Officer I have been honored to know. When we met in Jerusalem in the previous millennium, she was Hadassah Ben-Yishai, a little-known teacher of very great soul, who is long since passed on. During my ten-year mentorship and friendship, I was privileged to witness more of God and His ways in action than I ever imagined possible.

Ultimately, of course, all this was made possible by Father and Himself made visible through He who we know as Jesus, who claimed me and hopefully claimed you. And too God as Spirit, the Spirit of Truth who is so humbly present among us to fill us with life and move us to more. To God, my rock, my magnetic north and my only, I can't possibly say enough thankyous for having rocked my world with love, compassion, truth, and many more moments of Your glorious holiness than I deserve. Thy will be done now and forevermore.

ABOUT THE AUTHOR

Dr. Eliyahu (*eh-lee-YAH-who*) Lotzar has strived to bring hope and catalyze growth, helping many resolve tensions of self and group. For Lotzar, work is *avodah*, the Hebrew concept that encompasses work, stewardship, devotion, worship, acts of service, and the process of growth. His main vehicle for *avodah* is Reframed Reality, an organizational consultancy he founded and operates (https://reframedreality.com).

He was set on this trajectory of reframing-as-service when he was eight, when the Ancient of Days revealed some of Himself to Eliyahu. This profound and miraculously gracious moment infused in him a knack for seeing larger perspectives and a focus on how people relate to themselves, each other, and God.

Lotzar holds a Doctorate in Executive Leadership from St. John Fisher University, a Masters in Social Work from the Hebrew University of Jerusalem, and a Bachelors in Political Philosophy from James Madison College at Michigan State

University. His direction-setting doctoral research into employee soft skills and organizational culture has been accessed by commercial ventures, educational institutions, governments, and military agencies in over 130 countries.

He and his wife live amidst the gentle hills of northern Virginia, grateful to God for the beauty of this precious life.

Blessed is the Lord God, who gives and takes away and gives yet more.

www.ingramcontent.com/pod-product-compliance
Lightning Source LLC
Chambersburg PA
CBHW050557170426
43201CB00011B/1725